STANDING TALL

ANDY REID

STANDING TALL

**THE TALIBAN
NEARLY KILLED ME...
BUT THEY COULDN'T
TAKE AWAY MY
FIGHTING SPIRIT.
THIS IS MY
INSPIRATIONAL
STORY**

JOHN BLAKE

Published by John Blake Publishing Ltd,
3 Bramber Court, 2 Bramber Road,
London W14 9PB, England

www.johnblakepublishing.co.uk

www.facebook.com/Johnblakepub facebook
twitter.com/johnblakepub twitter

First published in hardback in 2013; this revised paperback edition published 2014

ISBN: 978-1-78219-746-1

British Library Cataloguing-in-Publication Data:

A catalogue record for this book is available from the British Library.

Design by www.envydesign.co.uk

Printed in Great Britain by CPI Group (UK) Ltd

1 3 5 7 9 10 8 6 4 2

Papers used by John Blake Publishing are natural, recyclable products made from
wood grown in sustainable forests. The manufacturing processes conform to the
environmental regulations of the country of origin.

Every attempt has been made to contact the relevant copyright-holders,
but some were unobtainable. We would be grateful if the
appropriate people could contact us.

'An honest, hard-hitting and sometimes terrifying account of something most of us will never experience, written by one of the hardest, bravest and nicest men I've ever met. Makes Andy McNab seem like Andy Pandy (please don't tell Andy McNab I said that...!)'

Jason Manford

DEDICATION

I would like to dedicate this book to my Nan, Ellen Reid, who passed away in 2012. She was an amazing lady whose strength, values and kindness will stay with me forever.

CONTENTS

FOREWORD BY SI KING AND DAVE MYERS,   XI
THE HAIRY BIKERS

FOREWORD BY MAJOR GENERAL   XIII
SIR EVELYN WEBB-CARTER, KCVO, OBE, DL

ACKNOWLEDGEMENTS   XVII

CHAPTER 1: WAKING UP   1

CHAPTER 2: CHILDHOOD   11

CHAPTER 3: HOSPITAL   25

CHAPTER 4: ARMY LIFE   37

CHAPTER 5: KOSOVO AND IRAQ   61

CHAPTER 6: AFGHANISTAN   71

CHAPTER 7: FIGHTING THE TALIBAN   87

CHAPTER 8: LOSING MATES   105

CHAPTER 9: HANDJAR   119

CHAPTER 10: THE DAY THAT CHANGED   131
EVERYTHING

CHAPTER 11: KARL'S STORY   141

CHAPTER 12: CLAIRE'S STORY   149

CHAPTER 13: REHAB, THE PARADE AND   159
THE PARACHUTE

CHAPTER 14: THE MILLIES   183

CHAPTER 15: STANDING TALL   193

POSTSCRIPT: FOR WILLIAM   201

FOREWORD BY SI KING AND DAVE MYERS, THE HAIRY BIKERS

We both agree that this is one of the most honest, heartwarming and inspirational books we have ever read. It is the story of an extraordinary human being, Andy Reid.

The book takes you on a journey that is everyone's worst nightmare. Andy takes the reader to Afghanistan in an honest account about what life is like for our soldiers and how it feels to be in battle on the front line. It's fascinating and not without a few laughs, but just when Andy is about to return home to his fiancée, tragedy strikes and Andy loses his legs and one of his arms. What follows is the story of one man's courageous, inspirational battle to rebuild his life and his future – and that of his fiancée and closest family members. Andy describes with real honesty the darkest times as well as the times of pride and joy, and how one human being can rebuild his life and be a rock for those around him. If anyone out there takes our soldiers for granted, this book will make them think again.

Andy and Claire, we salute you both and wish you all the best. Congratulations, Andy, on a wonderful book.

Si King and Dave Myers

Afghanistan. Andy tells a good tale and I have heard him speak in public on the theme that as one chapter closes another opens with new opportunities. From what I have seen of him in these last two years has proved to me that he has grasped those new opportunities with a relish and determination that would be hard to beat. This book is a shining example of just such an opportunity.

Evelyn Webb-Carter

ACKNOWLEDGEMENTS

I would like to acknowledge the men I worked alongside in Afghanistan in the summer of 2009 of the 2nd Battalion, The Royal Regiment of Fusiliers. It was my pleasure to work and fight with these men, especially Sergeant Simon Valentine and Private Shaun Bush who made the ultimate sacrifice.

I would also like to acknowledge the men from 3rd Battalion The Yorkshire Regiment (Duke of Wellington's) who also paid the ultimate price in the summer of 2009: Private Jonathan Young, Corporal Liam Riley and Lance Corporal Graham Shaw. I draw great strength from their loss; the fact that I am still here despite my injuries makes me very lucky and out of respect for them I will never stop moving forward.

CHAPTER 1

WAKING UP

'Put out the light! Put out that fucking light!'
The voice was raw, terrified, almost hysterical and quite clearly my own. I heard it just after my head had suddenly lit up with a piercing, blazing lance of light that burned through my eyes like white hot acetylene. Somebody has since told me that the words remind them of a line from Shakespeare. Apparently some black dude called Othello says them – OK, some of them anyway – just before he strangles his wife. I know how he felt; if I could have got my hands on the stupid bastards who were shining what seemed like a bloody searchlight in my face I would have strangled them myself.

I am a soldier, I hate light. I much prefer to skulk

around in the darkness unseen and unheard. If I am caught in the open by the unexpected burst of light from a Schermuly rocket or a trip flare then my instinct and training tell me to get the hell out; leg it into cover; dig in with my eyelids if necessary. Do whatever I can to get into the safety of the shadows.

All I was aware of was this piercing, blinding incandescence filling my head. What was going on? I became aware that there were people in the background, vague silhouettes behind the glare. Who were they? They must be looking for me. Had I been seen? Was there about to be a sudden bone-shattering, flesh-tearing burst of gunfire, or worse still a rocket grenade? I felt something well up in my chest and realised it was panic. For the first time in my life I felt real fear. It filled my mouth like the after-taste of cold sick, and caught in my throat so that when I tried to cry out again I coughed and spluttered.

Someone grabbed my shoulder. I tried to push whoever it was away but for some reason I couldn't move my arm; in fact I could not move anything. All I could do was to snarl and spit up at them like a tethered pit bull.

Mercifully they backed off and the light extinguished as quickly as it had appeared. I lay back, barely breathing, waiting for another attack. A maniac was now beating shit out of a bass drum in my head. If my heart went any faster I felt sure it would burst out of my chest. I had to concentrate hard as I listened for the slightest sound. I had fought off one of them but they would surely try again? Or were they hanging back, looking to pick me off at long range. Was I even now in somebody's cross hairs?

Slowly, gradually, my fear subsided like a hard-on in a draught. I was completely goosed, on my chinstraps, unable to move. What was wrong? All I could do was lie there, hoping I was safe, that someone from the base would soon come and find me. In the meantime I had to keep quiet, if I made a noise they would be on me for sure.

I must have dozed, because I jerked back to consciousness with a grunt. How long had I been here? I was thirsty, hot and my head still throbbed as if I had mainlined Jagerbombs all night. Then slowly the pins and needles in my brain began to ease, the flashing lights and discordant sounds began to make some sense. I started to take note of where I was. A strange, antiseptic smell pervaded the air, so different from the stench of dust, cowshit and rotting vegetables that I was used to. It was dark apart from a dim light that shone through the slats of a drawn blind casting a calming pattern on a clean white wall. I moved and felt the cool rustle of crisp cotton sheets.

Thank fuck! I was in a bed and I felt that sudden surge of relief the troubled sleeper has when he awakens from a nightmare. Then came the click of a door handle being cautiously opened and I froze; plunged back for an instant again into the sheer terror of the light. The door opened. Despite the gloom I was able make out someone standing in the threshold.

My breath caught in my throat as I stifled a sob. I had recognised her in an instant. There, now, walking to the bedside was my Claire. Her spirit, the vision of her, had been my constant off-duty companion for the last three months of my deployment. Every night as I waited for sleep, every day as I sat, catching a snatched moment of reflection during busy operations, we would meet up in my head and chat together. I would imagine and remember: the softness of her hair, the warm scent of her neck, the way she laughed at my jokes. Now here she was, in the flesh and in my room and I knew now that this was not a dream.

Following her came two more people equally welcome, so that in place of fear and terror now round my bed stood the three most important people in my life: my Claire, my mother and my old man. I started to laugh then cry uncontrollably. The relief that I was not after all lying in the dark out in the field was so great that even when a doctor appeared and admitted to being the stupid git who had shone a torch in my eyes, I was pleased to see him as well.

I lay back and let memory seep back into my mind like the incoming tide. I now remembered: I was in Selly Oak hospital in Birmingham; I was in the military wing; I was safe; I was not in pain and I was very happy. But I knew the feeling of happiness was an artificial one. It was a drowsy, sugar-coated hallucination, like you get with a lot of booze and fags; a creation of the morphine that was flowing into me by a plastic tube. Of course I was delighted to be with the three people I loved the most but it could not totally bury my desolation at the loss of three other companions who had been even closer to me. They were now gone and I missed them terribly. My left and right legs and my right arm were 6,000 miles away. I had left them somewhere in Afghanistan, lost forever – bloody careless or what!

At about 06:00 hours on Tuesday 13 October 2009, near Forward Operating Base (FOB) Nolay, Helmand Province, Afghanistan, I was blown up by a Taliban-manufactured pressure plate improvised explosive device (IED). What was left of me was evacuated back to the UK that evening in a specially fitted out Boeing C17 Globemaster. Compared to a Jumbo, a Globemaster does not look very comfortable but let me assure you that the service on board is second to none. British Airways might boast that they take more care of you but I doubt that they can match the care available on that flight. Not for me a glass of warm complimentary champagne and a meal that tastes of sawdust. On this flight, in the care of a Critical Care Air Support Team (CCAST), I was literally kept alive. Due to their success I made it to the specialist military wing of Selly Oak hospital in Birmingham at eight o'clock on the morning of 14 October, only 26 hours after my injury. My parents and Claire were waiting for me and stayed with me in my room until that hapless doctor shone a light in my eyes, woke me up, and I told everybody to piss off.

I say I 'woke up'. It took a nearly two days before I really came to my senses. I had been heavily sedated which made my confusion over the light in my eyes so much worse. Apparently when Claire first saw me I did not know who she was and I started kicking off, shouting at everyone including my parents. As far as I was concerned I was still on patrol in Afghanistan and now there were apparent strangers looking down at me while I was completely exposed and helpless. The doctors had to tell my family to leave the room and warned them that the next 24 hours were critical; the chances were that I might not make it. Those were very dire moments for Claire and my parents.

Now that I had calmed down and realised where I was and what had happened and memory started to come back to me, the doctor explained in more detail what my injuries were. I was not shocked when he said that I had lost my legs; the mental image of looking down when I got blown up and not being able to see them was now stuck in my mind.

The next day I went into theatre and when I came out they removed the tube that was assisting my breathing. Claire and my parents were, again, waiting for me outside Critical Care. My nurse, who I learned was called Kate, had fetched them onto the ward. I was so happy to see Claire once more, to see them all, that

I tried to embrace them... but with what? My dad stood there, clearly distressed at watching my pathetic writhing, desperate to make his own gesture, so he started patting my head and rubbing my hair, since there was not a lot else of me left to grab hold of.

He had never done this before. In fact nobody had ever done this to me before and I was struck at how bloody weird it felt. I shouted out to him: 'Pack it in Dad, I'm not a fucking dog!' There was a brief embarrassed silence and then we all burst out laughing; my recovery had begun.

On 20 October, because the doctors felt that my progress had been so good, I was moved onto a ward, Ward S4. That is where all the lads go to after Critical Care. Hardly luxury though; you get put in a six-man bay with only curtains separating the beds. However, I just saw it as another step closer to getting home. That soon became my abiding obsession. Despite the standard of care and the kindness of the nurses all I wanted to do was to get out of hospital as soon as I could and get home to Claire.

A number of people have asked me why I decided to begin my story waking up in the hospital and not with the explosion. The answer is simple. The IED was not the beginning of the story; if it was anything it was the end. Let me explain. As a highly trained section commander who knows his Army Methods of Instruction manual backwards, I know that if I am to try and tell you a story then, like anything else you do in the army, it needs to first of all have a clear aim and then a proper beginning, middle and an end.

My aim when I started writing this book was simple: to tell my story. But then I realised that there are two stories to tell. The first is the story of 25068908 Corporal William Andrew Reid, Burma Company, 3rd Battalion the Yorkshire Regiment: Infantry Section Commander. And then there is the story of Andy Reid, triple amputee sky diver, cyclist and charity fund raiser, winner of the 2010 *Sun* Military Award, soon to be husband and now author.

In both stories the IED is not the beginning. It was the end of Corporal Reid's story and whilst the shattered remains of him were shipped back to UK that might have been it, but then that doctor shone his light in the ward at Selly Oak and the broken and torn body woke up. Andy Reid was born.

But telling you the stories of these two people is not the only reason I am writing this book. The legacy of Iraq and Afghanistan is going to be a generation of maimed and damaged young men, and that will have many profound implications. On the positive side, as some wag has already observed, we should have a bloody world-beating Paralympic team, but on the downside there are – and there are going to be a lot more – young guys and girls who now face a lifetime of pain, disability and impairment. They will have to fight hard just to do those little daily acts like taking a piss and having a shower that you lot find easy, let alone the difficult things like getting laid and finding a job. Your charity and understanding are going to be needed for many years to come.

Yet I am not seeking your pity for people like me; I am not even seeking your admiration at how tough and resilient we have all been. But what I do want you to understand and appreciate is that we are a direct consequence of Government policy. Our shattered minds and bodies result from operations conducted in their name.

I am a soldier. I make no comment on whether the strategy of the British Government is right or wrong; that is your call. But I want you to know, as much as someone who has not been there or been through it themselves can ever know, what operations in Afghanistan are like, what happens to those who get injured and what future they might have. Then you must make up your own mind.

CHAPTER 2

CHILDHOOD

I was born on 21 September 1976 in Birkenhead on the Wirral Peninsular and was christened William Andrew Reid. William is a family name that my dad insisted upon but as far as my mum was concerned I was Andrew from the start. Having had a lot of time recently to think about my early life it has occurred to me that if there is an ideal upbringing and training for someone destined to become a triple amputee, then arguably I have had it.

My preparation started when I was five. My dad was a mad keen motorcyclist; still is in fact. In those days he used to ride a big BSA Gold Star, and in order to carry us around, added a sidecar combination. You hardly see them nowadays but back then it was great. I used to imagine I was flying as I zoomed along, so close to the ground, in the bullet-shaped compartment. One day, Dad took us for a spin and I was in there with my mum and my three sisters. It was great fun being snuggled up together. However, the fun turned into a nightmare when we were hit side on by a car. It was no fault of my dad's; in fact it later transpired that the driver of the car was drunk. I really hope he had a bastard hangover because what he did to us was devastating.

Dad was lucky and managed to walk away with cuts and bruises; so did my younger sister but my older sister suffered a broken pelvis, and my right leg was broken in three places. But the worst injured was poor Mum. Her right ankle had been completely crushed in the impact. That terrible injury dominated the rest of my childhood.

For years Mum suffered a series of painful operations and eventually she had to have the joint frozen and immobilised. It was awful for her, she could hardly walk and life was very difficult. When I was ten she went back into hospital to see if there was anything they could do. There was. I remember going to see her and finding her very tearful. She explained that the surgeons had just told her that the only way they could improve her mobility was to amputate her leg just below the knee. I recall her telling us that it was not so bad and would mean that she would not have to be way from us so much having treatment.

She had the operation and was fitted with a

prosthetic foot. So, when I suffered my own injuries I was no stranger to the demands that it places upon the injured and their families, and I also had a pretty good idea of the demands it would place upon me. In particular, adapting to the loss of my right arm was considerably helped by my previous experiences. Losing the use of your right hand, even temporarily, is no joke, especially for a young, growing lad. Writing and performing other functions with the left hand can take some getting used to I can tell you. Fortunately I had had previous experience of a similar loss having broken my right arm twice when I was at school.

The first time it was my sister's fault. I was only 11 and we were in her school messing about in a room used for drying washing. I was stood on a radiator and above my head were a series of pipes running the length of the room just below the ceiling, so you could swing from one side of it to the other using them as monkey bars. My sister bet me that I couldn't make it across without letting go, and I was dead sure that I could. I was pretty athletic even then, playing rugby league, cross-country and mountain biking. So this would be a doddle.

She grinned slyly and told me to try. I leapt off the radiator in true Tarzan style and grabbed the first pipe. Now forget Tarzan and think Tom and Jerry instead. The bloody pipe was red hot (as had been the radiator, I later remembered) and the instant I grasped it I let go with a scream of pain. I now took on the aerodynamic properties of a sack of potatoes and fell to the ground landing on my right wrist which snapped like a twig in a car crash. My sister swore me to secrecy on pain of death and tried to hide my injury from our dad when he came to take me home. Of course he spotted something was wrong at once; probably something to do with my chalky face and whimpered moans. She attempted to explain it all away by telling him that I had simply fallen over whilst messing about contrary to her specific instructions. Nice one, Sis!

Later, in my teens, I fell off a table in a local youth club under circumstances that need not detain us further, and again broke my right arm. So when it came to losing it completely, at least I remembered that I could use my left hand for most of the important things in life.

However, some activities still piss me off, like trying to put toothpaste on my toothbrush. I lie the tooth-brush down then try to squeeze the paste on, and nine times out of every ten the fucking brush falls over. Another real pain is trying to fasten the zip on my jacket. You try it one-handed and I guarantee it will really get on your tits.

But, apart from those irritating little niggles, when I realised that I had lost my limbs I just thought, well, they are gone, so I just have to get on with it. I knew it was going to be hard and frustrating but I suppose in some ways, in view of what has happened to me, I was lucky to have had that prior insight. I was certainly lucky with my mum. Her example of being able to come to terms with and overcome her injury has inspired me to overcome mine. Any time I felt things were getting on top of me and that I really could not cope, I would think of Mum and remember her words: 'If I can hack this, so can you.'

I would like to say that I loved school and was a model pupil but that would be a bloody lie. Matters were not helped by the accident which meant that me and my sisters often went to stay with relatives while my mum went into hospital. Eventually my sister qualified for a place at a state boarding school but I was not so lucky and attended any number of schools until I was eventually sent to Rainford High School in St Helens where we had come to live, as my dad had a job as a projectionist at the local Savoy Cinema. Rainford High School's big claim to fame is that it was the school that the Oscar-nominated playwright Willy Russell attended – him of *Educating Rita* and *Shirley Valentine* fame. Apparently the real Shirley Valentine was a girl in his class who he had the 'hots' for but never had the courage to say so. Anyway, sadly I was not quite as successful as him and was asked to leave after three years and went off to finish my schooling at a place called Broadway High. This was an amalgamation of a number of technical schools and I was, at last, able to find some-thing I liked doing in the woodwork and metalwork classes. My main interest, however, was rugby football. Not that poncey nonsense played down in Twickenham, but rugby league. It is a passion that has stayed with me all my life.

As soon as I was able I left school without any real qualifications, because I had decided that I was going to become a soldier. I can't remember when I decided to join the army or why. All I do know is that as soon as I was 16 and able to sign up I headed for the recruiting office. To get into the army you need to prove three things: that you are not a dangerous criminal, that you are fit enough to train, and that you have at least *something* between the ears. I was pretty confident on passing the first two hurdles but after my poor showing at school was nervous about the last one. However, I was reassured that if it was the infantry I was after then the level required was not that high. It was 'grunts' they were looking for not rocket scientists. So, you can imagine my surprise then deep disappointment when I was turned down, not for my intelligence test result but on medical grounds. I was, perversely, underweight!

I was very disappointed, as were my parents. My friend's uncle was a serving soldier in the Queen's Lancashire Regiment and my old man called him up for some advice as to what to do. He suggested what, at the time, seemed a brilliant plan. He told me to get up early, drink nine pints of water, then go straight round to the recruiting office as soon as it opened. I would be first in, get weighed, then go for a piss; job done. I did as he said. Have you ever tried to drink nine pints of water in one go? It is bloody difficult. I have since learned that to force people to drink so much is a form of torture that was much favoured by the Spanish Inquisition! I am not bloody surprised. Your stomach swells and you can feel the fluid sloshing around like a washing machine as you walk. I waddled in through the recruiting office door like a space hopper on legs and managed to wedge myself into a chair and waited. The sergeant poked his head out of the door.

'Sorry mate, there will be a slight delay, you alright to hold on?'

By now my bladder had ballooned like a crash bag. I managed a smile through gritted teeth and nodded. He disappeared and I was left in agony. Sweat was starting to break out on my forehead and I suddenly realised that if I didn't go to the loo immediately I would literally explode in a welter of piss. I staggered into the cubicle and let go a veritable torrent that seemed to go on for hours. When I came out the wretched sergeant appeared and I was sent in to be weighed. I was exactly the same as before, 9 stone 5 pounds. I had failed again. They were very kind and gave me some good tips as to what sort of training I should do and sent me on my way.

Despondent, I went home and back to the job as a fork-lift truck driver I had sort of drifted into after leaving school. There I stayed, making occasional further attempts at joining up but meeting the same resistance. Then one day I was driving round the yard moving pallets. It was just after my 21st birthday and my dad had been going on about how 21 was the key of the door; the beginning of your life as an adult; and how I needed to think about what I was going to do, where I was going in life. Then it suddenly struck me that I had already made the decision. Here I was, trundling around a yard moving pallets. I did it 9 to 5 and then went home to me mum for tea, and on Friday and Saturday I went out for a beer and a laugh with my mates and maybe we would take in a St Helens game or whatever.

I stopped the truck and looked out through the windscreen and sort of saw that future stretching ahead of me; driving round and round in circles; moving pallets from here to there and then back again. It all seemed so boring and pointless. I had to do something else, get away, look for a life beyond the M6. A couple of months later I returned to the recruiting office. I had spent the intervening time doing some proper work-outs and following a high protein diet. This time I was determined to get in. However, in the intervening time the St Helens recruiting office had closed, so I would have to travel to Liverpool to join up. This was good, as Liverpool is the home town of the King's Regiment, my uncle's mob. At the St Helens railway station I realised that I was out of fags then I checked the price of a fare to Liverpool: bastard! I didn't have enough money for the fare *and* a packet of fags.

I pondered my options. The packet of fags was essential; the trip to Liverpool was not. I could buy the fags and still afford a fare to Wigan where there was another recruiting office. Off to Wigan I went and arrived at the office where I was welcomed by the cheery Recruiting Sergeant. I was impressed by his garish red sash, brightly coloured brassard and shiny shoulder titles, but when I read them I saw that they did not read 'Kings', instead they read 'QLR'. The Queen's Lancashire Regiment, abbreviated to QLR (or Queen's Last Resort as some comics call them) was the infantry regiment local to Wigan. I had, sort of, set my heart on the Kings but I had no money to go elsewhere, QLR it would have to be. But at least my determination and persistence had paid off, as it always does if you stick to what you want. I was in the army at last.

I said at the beginning of this chapter that I was a section commander. A section is the basic manoeuvre unit in the British army. It consists of eight men: a commander, normally a full corporal; his 2IC, normally a lance corporal; and six riflemen. Three sections make a platoon, three platoons make a company and three companies (with administrative and support companies added on) make a battalion.

What happens after that only gods and generals know; that is as far as I have gone in the great scheme of things. Anyway, in my view section commander is the hardest command of all. Ranks above the section commanders are required to try and keep out of the battle because they have to observe what is going on, decide on their plan and give the appropriate orders. A section commander, however, is part of the fighting force of his section. He has to command his blokes as well as having to fire and manoeuvre with them as a rifleman. It is for this reason that the hardest compulsory course in the military, in terms of the demands it makes on the fitness and determination of the student, is the Army Section Commander's Battle Course which is run at the Infantry Battle School based in Brecon in South Wales.

This course is designed to train young Non Commissioned Officers (NCOs) to be section commanders and to reinforce how hard a job that is. All training is done with the student's personal kit and webbing loaded down to represent operational holdings of rations and ammunition. All the platoon weapons are carried and everything is done at full pace, and the enemy are always uphill. Just to make things that much more interesting, the training is carried out in the Brecon Beacons which seem to have their own micro-climate that blows in direct from hell.

Let me tell you that hell does not need great heat to inflict its misery. It can do that just as easily by creating a cold, wet and dreary desolation that soaks you by day and then freezes you by night. However, sometimes it does decide to show you its fiery temper. Usually it reserves it for the dreaded 'Fan Dance', a timed forced march across Corn Dhu, Pen y Fan and Cribben – the three Brecon Beacons. Then it turns on the heat: you have to run up the steep slopes weighed down with kit, your boots slipping on the dry tussock grass. Webbing chafes the skin from the body so that the salt of the sweat pouring out of you makes the raw flesh burn. Your brain begins to broil under your helmet like a chicken in a pressure cooker, and all the while the directing staff are running round as if their hair is on fire, shouting in your ear, driving you on, attacking any weakness that they see. I did Junior Brecon when I was over 30. I had to compete against guys ten years younger, so it was particularly hard for me.

The experience changed my perceptions of what I wanted to do in the army. Up till then I had always found training pretty easy. In particular, because I had made efforts to get myself properly prepared physically, I found recruit training challenging but great fun. For the first 12 weeks after I joined I was based at Glencourse in Scotland for phase one recruit training. Then I moved to Catterick to complete the 10-week combat infantryman course. During this period I was amazed at how many of my fellow recruits were totally unprepared for the physical challenges that army training set them.

You would have thought that somebody who had volunteered to join the army, and in particular the infantry, would understand that it probably entailed getting up early in the morning, cleaning both your-self and your block, making you and your kit look smart, and a fair amount of hard physical exercise. Yet large numbers of recruits turned up and seemed genuinely surprised to discover that this was what was expected of them. I was astonished at how many had, apparently, never seen six o'clock in the morning before or who had never run further than 20 metres.

Also there were huge numbers who seemed to have relied entirely upon their mothers to carry out virtually every personal action for them, from washing their 'shreddies' (underpants) to wiping their arses. The result was that quite a few fell by the wayside until there were only a small number of us that eventually passed out and proceeded to our battalions.

In my case, the 1st Battalion The Queen's Lancashire Regiment was based in Lisanelly Barracks in Omagh, Northern Ireland. I arrived there in June 1998. Does that date mean anything to you? Let me remind you: earlier that year, at Easter, the Good Friday Agreement had been concluded followed by the Belfast Treaty. The Provisional IRA declared hostilities to be at an end and the whole fucking shooting match that was British military operations in Northern Ireland, first begun back in 1969, was starting to be dismantled. As a result, whilst we had plenty to do in carrying out joint patrols with the RUC, we did not face the threat which previously forced the army to keep a low profile. We were allowed into town as long as we only frequented the main shopping centres, kept out of the pubs, wore civilian clothes, and kept in groups of at least four.

I can remember one incident, when on Saturday 15 August 1998, four of us went in to buy some washing powder, starch and other essentials which the bloody NAAFI used to charge a profiteering price for. We finished our buying early and were heading back for a couple of pints before lunch and then an afternoon watching Sky Sports, when suddenly there came what I can only describe as an unearthly bang followed by an eerie silence. A plume of smoke appeared above the town. Not waiting for any more, we hurried back to Camp where we were told to get into uniform and report to our company lines. There we learned that a huge car bomb had been detonated in the centre of the town and there had been many casualties.

The Camp was designated as an impromptu morgue and I was one of those detailed to assist in taking bodies from the ambulances and other vehicles that had come from the town centre into the gymnasium where they were laid out for identification. It was a sight that still sticks like a screensaver in the back of my mind. There were all sorts of casualties: men, women and children, some missing limbs. Most were severely burned and many had bits of glass and masonry embedded in their flesh. The sights and the sheer brutality of it all sickened me. What sort of crazy mad fuck would want to deliberately inflict this sort of horror on innocents? It was my first experience of shattered bodies.

Yup, if anyone was brought up to be blown apart, it was me.

CHAPTER 3

HOSPITAL

People always ask me about pain. Was it painful when I got blown up? Was it painful when I awoke in hospital? The ones who seem most concerned by the answers are serving soldiers. No prizes for guessing why. I was the same. What would it be like to get blown up? Would you be able to hack it? Everybody is impressed by the wounded warrior who is able to rise above their injuries and make some form of life for themselves, but what if the whole experience simply reduced you to a blubbering wreck? Well I hope I can be encouraging when I say that there was no pain as far as I can remember, either immediately after the explosion or when I woke up in Selly Oak. What I do recall is feeling very, very tired; very, very sleepy. I knew that if I gave in to that drowsiness I was lost. Sleep may seem to offer a solace, it does not; it is the way to death. Whenever I felt sleepy, I got up and did something to make myself wake up in case I found that I never did.

Another thing I am often asked about is the phenomenon of phantom limbs. This is where you imagine that you still have a fully functioning arm or leg even though quite clearly it no longer exists. For example, as I write this I can easily imagine myself doing so with my right hand using a pen on paper. I can feel the movements of my hand and arm across the page, feel the pressure as my fingers grip the pen, and yet nothing is happening apart from some twitching in the stump that was my right arm. Apparently this will remain with me for life although it does subside with time. It is particularly prevalent in amputees like me who lose their limbs later in life.

The first time I was aware of it was at Selly Oak. It was part of the general recovery of my senses to the extent that I recognised people and remembered who they were and how much I loved them. You have got to understand that this is not a sudden process. You do not immediately switch from being spaced out on drugs and adrenalin to super-focused. It comes and goes. Sometimes you are right on the button, know exactly what is going on, and can carry on a sensible conversation. On other occasions you are on the bridge of the *Starship Enterprise*.

Another question that everybody wants to ask me –

normally only my mates feel brave enough to actually put it into words – is whether there has been any damage to the old wedding tackle. Don't worry, it was my first question after being blown up and I was assured that it all looked OK which, mercifully, has proved to be the case. I often used to think that whoever designed the human body made an error leaving such valuable bits dangling between the legs, just crying out to be shot away. However, they are, in fact, quite neatly protected and very fortunately many blokes who suffer bomb blasts to the legs like I have get to keep their Crown Jewels. Losing two legs is bad enough but to lose the third would be really hard to take, so one must be thankful for small mercies.

I say small mercies, however, one little-known – and about the only welcome – side-effect of an amputation is that it increases the size of your old man. Although large bits of your body have disappeared, apparently you still have the same amount of blood coursing through the veins and this, like 12 pints of Stella in a tight bladder, is desperate to force its way into any extremity you have left. This means that your todger gets far more blood pumped into it than it does when you have all your bits intact. In fact rumour has it that this explains why Admiral Nelson became such a randy sod after he lost his arm.

This blood business, however, is not all fun and games. After I had moved out of Critical Care I was lying in the bed on S4 Ward. One arm was wrapped in a big bandage and the other secured in a blue sling strapped up and elevated. I had a feeding tube down my throat giving me extra energy and all in all I was as trussed up as tight as a Christmas turkey. Suddenly I started to sweat as my body temperature shot up. Besides giving you a bigger todger, having so much blood but fewer places for it to go plays havoc with your temperature control system. In an entire person the blood is able to cool the body down by going out to the toes and fingers where the blood vessels are close to the skin's surface and heat can be lost more easily. But I had no toes and only a couple of fingers, so the blood could not cool down and I started to boil up inside. Sweat began to sluice out of me like juice out of a crushed melon. It drove me crazy just lying there, not being able to do anything about it. I couldn't wipe my forehead or even scratch my nuts. As for having a shit or a pee, forget it. Looking back, I think this was my lowest point. I had always been very independent and was proud of my self-sufficiency. Yet now I could not do even the most simple and intimate tasks for myself. My state of mind plummeted and I began to wish that the Taliban bomber had been better at his job and finished me off completely. Not being able to do anything was really getting me down and I felt useless and unwanted.

'Is this it from now on?' I raged. 'If I can do fuck-all for myself I would rather not bother with being here at all if this is all that I have to look forward to.' That afternoon a hand specialist came to see me about my remaining hand. I have not been very fair to my left hand so far and have failed to explain that the bomb had almost severed the index finger. To begin with, the surgeons simply grafted it back on to the stump almost as a cosmetic exercise rather than trying to do anything serious with it. The specialist was almost irritatingly upbeat.

'Don't worry, Andy,' she breezed. 'We can save your index finger – but you won't be able to use it for at least two weeks.'

By that stage I had had enough. I glared at her. She seemed a bit surprised. No doubt she was expecting me to burst into applause at her welcome news. Instead I had a bit of a fit.

'Fuck off!' I announced. 'Why don't you just cut it off?'

She was taken aback but I was now into my stride. I gestured to the offending digit with my head.

'I can't be arsed with any more bloody surgery. I don't need it anyway, what use would I have for it for anything?'

The specialist was hurt and upset, I could see that. She got up from her chair, apologised quietly and left. Thank God that Claire was in the room to witness this nonsense. She immediately pitched into me and told me off.

I started to cry. I was at rock bottom and had come to the end of my reserves of strength. Claire was desperately worried. She comforted me as best she could and then went to find my Welfare Officer, Sergeant

Major Lister. Together they laid their plans, and later that night they came to see me. One I could handle, but faced with both of them I was overwhelmed. They talked me round and the next day I apologised to the specialist and we had the operation. Thank God we did; losing the finger would have been bloody stupid. Now I have a properly operating hand. I might not be able to make a full fist, so a career as a fast-jabbing boxer is out of the question, but I can hold a pint of Stella!

Once my hand was sorted, the rehab could start in earnest. My first aim was Remembrance Day 2009. This was fast approaching and I had made it clear that I wanted to play as full a part in it as I could. In particular, it was suggested that we used the event to reunite me with the members of my patrol at the Warminster barracks, the one I had left prematurely and without permission courtesy of the Taliban IED. This was unfinished business for me. I was the patrol commander so it was my responsibility to make sure they all made it safely back. They were all much younger than I was. Out of the seven the oldest was only 22, and I felt very bad that I had left them leaderless. I was keen to see them all again. The doctor told me that if I wanted to go and see them I would have to be able to get out of a wheelchair onto the floor and then get back in it again without any help. Having been given the challenge, that was enough for me.

The next day I booked a physio session. I was told

that a young lady captain called Ann would be coming to see me with a view to teaching me how to sit up by myself. I decided that I would try and surprise her. When she arrived and pulled the curtains back, there I was sat up already.

'Good morning ma'am,' I said cheerfully. She said nothing. I followed up by asking whether we were going to the gym. She seemed genuinely shocked.

'Who helped you up?' she demanded.

'No one,' I replied.

She stared at me. Just to make the point I flopped back on my bed and then sat up again. She shook her head in disbelief but then made a decision.

'Right, get in your wheelchair and I will meet you in the physio room.'

This was what I needed. Something to get me motivated and give me a challenge. I headed down to the gym where Ann and an RAF physical training instructor called Dave were waiting for me. What followed was an exquisite form of torture. They sat me on one of those huge inflatable balls that you see in workout videos. Sounds pretty simple, and it is for anyone with two legs. However, imagine trying to perch a little child or a doll on one. That was effectively what I was trying to do. Keeping upright put a huge strain on my core muscles, the abdomen and the laterals. This would be important for when I was to start walking again.

I was able to manage to keep myself sitting up but only for about 20 seconds at a time, then I would come off balance. Dave suggested that doing it in front of a mirror might help. Without thinking I agreed and I was wheeled round to a part of the gym where there were full body mirrors set in the walls. Dave set up the ball and placed me on it. I turned to face the wall and almost cried out. This was the first time I had seen my body full-length in a mirror and it was quite a shock to see the stubby limbs and the sheer brutality of what was missing. It was like looking at a tree that had been hacked at by vandals looking for firewood. I suddenly felt sick. I called off the session and went back to my bed and sobbed myself to sleep.

When the day of the Remembrance Parade came I was obviously excited but the excitement was tinged with sadness. I was desperate to see the lads but I also knew that we would be remembering Private Young, who had died in Helmand. In order to get down to Warminster in time I had a very early start from Selly Oak. Claire had pointed out a day or so earlier that I had nothing to wear. Fortunately, the Corporals' Mess heard about the problem and bought me a suit. This was very good of them and it was the first of many kindnesses they extended to me. With no need for trouser legs or a right sleeve, at least it wouldn't have cost them that much!

I arrived in Warminster to find that the service was being held in one of the big vehicles garages that are a feature of Battlesbury Barracks. The service was just what I wanted: moving and very emotional. But being held in a draughty garage it was also freezing cold, blood supply or no blood supply. As I was being wheeled to the Sergeants' Mess afterwards one of the lads said it was cold enough to grow ice cream. I agreed. 'I can't feel my toes!' I quipped. He nodded and then gave me a quick look. We both burst out laughing. I have used that joke many times since and it is beginning to wear a bit thin, but it was bloody funny at the time.

We went into the mess and all my section were in there waiting for me. I cannot express how good it was to see them all again and how much it touched me. The last time we had been together was less than a month earlier, yet it seemed like an eternity in terms of where we were now. However, I was still their section commander. I was very close to tears and so were they – but we hid it well behind man hugs. Fortunately – or unfortunately – I was unable to drink anything due to my medication but they made up for it for me, and later that afternoon it was back to Selly Oak. For once I was happy to be there. It had become a sort of home and a sanctuary. Warminster had been fun but it had taken a lot out of me, and I realised then that getting better was going to be a long business.

This soon became even more apparent as I settled into a regime of doing as much physio as I could whilst waiting for my wounds to heal. I found sitting on the ward deadly, so I was constantly down in the gym. I used to get a bit fed up with some of the other lads who seemed to want to just hang about in bed, moaning and whinging. Fortunately, Claire was able to visit every day and quite often we would go out to the shops for a look around, but that was hard for me, as I had to sit in the front seat of the car watching her getting the wheelchair out of the boot. The chair was electric and even with the battery off it weighed about 60 pounds. Claire is no Arnold Schwarzenegger so watching her struggle with it when I used to be able to handle things like that with ease was killing me. I knew I had to get up on some new legs as fast as I could. I had to get to Headley Court.

Headley Court, home of the Defence Medical Rehabilitation Centre, is an Elizabethan manor house in Surrey. Formerly a rehabilitation centre run by the RAF, and the HQ for Canada's forces in Europe during World War Two, it is now the joint services rehabilitation facility. It has become a centre of excellence in the fitting and successful adoption of prosthetic limbs. I was desperate to get there and get up on some new legs – but my wounds had to be healed first.

Before we went to Afghanistan one of my best mates, Richie, was planning to get married and had asked me to be his best man. This was a massive honour; we had been friends for about nine years. When we got the call to go to Afghanistan he had to postpone the wedding. He was obviously gutted but he made plans to get married when we came back and the date was set for 28 November, but when I was injured he announced that

34

discipline of the special forces. Beards and straggly hair might now be allowed but weapon serviceability, fieldcraft and fire control are now more highly prized, and above all else is sleep.

Sleep is the most valuable commodity in the army when you are in the field. There is never enough of it and as operations progress you get less and less of it. It is prized above cigarettes, rations, even money. You learn to catnap but it is never enough. Your eyelids begin to feel as if they are weighted with shot. You start to hallucinate and you have to constantly slap yourself to keep awake. I have seen many people literally dead on their feet. I have even heard some snoring while marching along!

Ask a soldier what is the most beautiful sound in the world. You might expect him to say the sound of the regimental bugle call or his regimental march. Or he might say the staccato bark of machine gun fire, the crunch of boots on gravel or the massed bands on Horse Guards. If he was bit of a wazzer you might think he would say the sound of his wife's voice or his children's excited shrieks on Christmas morning. But if he was being truly honest the most beautiful sound a soldier ever hears is that rising buzzing tone the zip on his sleeping bag makes as it is drawn up to his chin and he can lie back and close those leaded lids and escape to the Land of Doss. (I can't speak for former female colleagues, but I'm sure they would have had similar thoughts.)

When I was growing up, there was a popular

recruiting slogan: 'Join the Army and See the World'. When I joined the Dukes, I learnt an alternative version: 'Join the Army and See the World, or Join the Dukes and Area Clean It'. 'Area cleaning' is a miserable chore which all soldiers soon become very familiar with. It is employed to keep the barrack area as clean and pristine as possible, particularly the parade ground, or 'God's Little Acre' as it is often referred to. This is not because the Big Man in Heaven has anything to do with it. It refers to the True Deity, the Supreme Being before whom all creation trembles: the Regimental Sergeant Major. He requires cleanliness in an instant, so first thing in the morning all those not on essential duties are formed into a long line that stretches from one side of the barracks to the other. On the order 'Advance!' we creep forward, eyes glued to the ground like Scotsmen looking for loose change, and we pick up every bit of debris we come across, be it fag ends or somebody's used bit of chewing gum. In the Dukes we seemed to do an inordinate amount of it wherever we were deployed, and nobody thanked us for it – and it was a long way from the dream of seeing the world promised by that recruiting poster.

However, despite the shrinking deployment of troops overseas other than on operations, the increased intensity of those operations, and other restrictions on time and money, the army is still not a bad place in which to see other parts of the world. Just by way of operational deployment you can find yourself in any of the NATO countries, much of the Middle East, and some interesting parts of the Far East, such as Borneo. And of course there is Afghanistan, where you can indulge that other well-worn corruption of the recruiting slogan: 'Join the Army and See the World: meet new, strange and interesting people and kill them'. In this respect, since the fall of the Berlin Wall, British troops have been able to do that in a number of interesting areas such as the Balkans and Iraq as well as Afghanistan. However, I suspect that everyone's appetite for that sort of global policing has now been satisfied and when, rather than if, we pull out of Afghanistan it will be a long time before we poke our nose in somewhere as confidently as we did back in 2002.

Even today, besides the obvious travel opportunities to the world hotspots, the army is keen to encourage its soldiers to seek to develop themselves, their leadership qualities and their character and personalities by what is termed 'Adventurous Training'. This is seen as a cheaper, and of course much safer, opportunity to stretch a soldier's abilities to survive in a hostile and demanding environment, and by using teamwork and cooperation achieve something worthwhile. If there can be a good public relations spin on it, so much the better.

Climbing Everest was an early but now slightly clichéd example of this. Subsequently, British soldiers have planned and executed all sorts of extraordinary expeditions and achieved remarkable feats of endurance. However, not everybody is cut out to be a Bear Grylls, and a number of perhaps less motivated individuals have spotted that if you use enough intelligence and guile you can turn the situation to your advantage. Essentially, if you can come up with a reasonable excuse for going somewhere exotic then you can usually work in a visit to a sun-kissed shore or a bar with a view that is normally only open to the mega-rich.

I had an early opportunity to sample this when I volunteered to join an expedition mounted by the Queen's Lancashire Regiment from Omagh. Officially the project had two aims. The first was to conduct a tour of the First World War battlefields on the Tanzanian and Kenyan border, and the second was to climb Mount Kilimanjaro. When I saw this trip advertised on BROs (Battalion Routine Orders) I thought this is just what I joined up for: see the world and have some adventure. The next day I reported to my Company 2IC, Lieutenant Crook, who was organising and leading the trip.

I told him how keen I was to do it, how I had the cash, and as I was single at the time it was not a drama to piss off for three weeks. The fact that, into the bargain, I would miss our company's turn on the guards and routing Camp duties rota, a period of unending boredom at the best of times, so much the better!

Before the trip we were to do some pre-training. This was to take place in the Lake District and most of the team were already there. Three of us – me, Jimmy Hardman and a mate called Smudge – were to travel there separately on the Larne Ferry which would take us to Stranraer in Scotland. At the time I was about 22 and had only been in the army around a year. We were all private soldiers but Jimmy took control, having been a lance corporal before he was bust back down to the ranks. Even so, he might have been the same rank as us but he was a pretty crazy guy and if Jimmy had a plan it was good for your health to go along with it. He was a hard man by name and by nature. I say 'was' because he is, alas, no longer with us. He passed away a few years ago but whilst I knew him, despite his reputation he was a top guy.

We got the ferry and all was going well. We had a laugh and a few beers and I thought this is great, I am getting paid to go to the Lakes for the weekend. When we docked at Stranraer the plan was to meet the others and drive to Ambleside where we were to be based. However, no one was there, nobody met us. This was, of course, before mobile phones were as widely available as they are today. Certainly none of us had one.

Jimmy took the lead and said: 'Right lads, let's go into that pub and wait.'

This was about 15:00 and we had a few more beers until by about 18:00 there was still no sign of the rest of the party and Jimmy decided that we would check in to the pub for the night and go out on the town. Jimmy was the boss, so we did as he said. We signed in, got changed and went out on the piss. We found a cracking nightclub and were giving it large when Lieutenant Crook and another member of the group suddenly turned up at around midnight. Apparently they had run into a plague of locusts or some other drama getting there. I was concerned lest our little tour break would get us into trouble but they were fine about it. All we had to make sure was that we were ready to leave for Ambleside at 09:00 the next morning.

Well that was fine then. I was so happy that it had all seemed to turn out well, that I had a few more drinks. In the course of doing so, as often happens, I lost the other lads. This was not at all unusual. It either meant that someone had pulled a bird or, more likely, had fallen into a hedge. Either way, that guardian angel that is said to look after children and drunks normally sees them safely home, eventually.

When I stumbled down to breakfast the next morning, Lieutenant Crook was there along with everybody else but of Jimmy there was no sign. The boss was not happy. We only had a weekend and had already missed a lot of valuable training time. He was desperate to get us all to the Lakes. He quizzed us closely as to Jimmy's whereabouts. He was sure one of us would know where he was but Jimmy was a free agent, quite capable of anything without resort to us. Suddenly the B&B owner stuck her head round the door. Did we know someone called Jimmy, she asked. Despite this being Scotland, and everybody being called Jimmy, we were so desperate we said, yes we did.

'Well,' she said, 'there's a fellow of that name on the phone now calling from Edinburgh.'

Edinburgh! What the fuck was he doing in Edinburgh?

I was never any great shakes at geography but even I realised that Edinburgh was about the furthest point one could get diametrically from Stranraer. This was about 10.30. When we spoke to him he assured us that he was on his way, but Edinburgh was easily a four-hour journey even in a fast car. The boss and his 2IC, Sergeant Hunter, did not take the news well. Jimmy was in deep shit. By the time he got back to us and then we travelled to Ambleside it would almost be time to pack up and come back.

Dolefully we ordered a cup of tea and settled down to wait. You can imagine our surprise when the door opened and in marched Jimmy as large as life and twice as ugly. He was completely at ease and hailed us as if nothing had happened.

'Where the fuck have you been Hardman, are you taking the piss?' Lieutenant Crook was in a direct mood.

'I was in the Edinburgh,' Jimmy answered; his expression as innocent as a novice nun. The boss tapped his watch.

'You couldn't have got from Edinburgh to here in that time, not even in bloody Concorde. It's the other side of the country.'

Jimmy gave a laugh. 'Sorry boss, I thought you understood. I've been in the Edinburgh Arms, it's about a hundred yards down the High Street from here.' I burst out laughing as did the rest of the lads. Even the boss had to grin – eventually.

So we got our stuff and set off for the Lakes, at last. When we arrived at the campsite we all booked in, got settled and had a brief about the next day. Then we went out into Ambleside for some scoff and a few drinks. Jimmy was gated as a punishment for his liberties of the previous night and was left to look after the site. In town, the night was going well and we were all getting to know each other. Again we managed to find a local nightclub. The bouncers were not keen on letting us in. This is a common situation for us squaddies, or at least it used to be. Local lads never appreciate having their women nicked off them by a group of fit, hot-blooded Toms, so they normally try and accuse us of being troublemakers and starting fights. We were wise to this and told them that we were looking for a bloke who had gone AWOL. They let us in and we were away.

At about two in the morning, just as even the rougher girls were looking sexy, the boss told us we were going. Reluctantly we piled into the minibus and set off back to the campsite. Unsay, the driver, had not been drinking but the roads around there are tight and very bendy with no street light at all. On a particularly winding stretch, Unsay lost control of the bus. He reckoned later that he must have hit some black ice. We went up a small bank at the side of the road and turned over. The bus landed on its side before skidding down the road for a few metres. Most of us had been dossing but we quickly woke up. Mercifully everyone was OK and we slid the door open and climbed out.

It was 02:30. Moreover it was January and we only had our pulling gear on: thin shirts and trousers. It was now bloody freezing and so the boss decided we should get the bus back on its wheels and view the damage. Astonishingly we managed it and in the dark the bus seemed serviceable so we all got back in. Then one of the lads announced that he could smell petrol. We may have been cold but not that cold so we all jumped out, put the four ways on and started walking back to Camp. Some of us went to a house we had passed down the road. We planned to ring the police. We knocked on the door. Understandably the occupants were very suspicious and we had to pass our military ID cards under the door to prove that we were not axe-wielding maniacs before they agreed to open up to us. The next day was spent sorting out the minibus and then we had to return to Omagh... no walking having been achieved!

All in all, during that weekend we had achieved nothing in the way of training but had made friendships that made the subsequent trip to Africa much easier. Sadly Jimmy did not make Tanzania. He was taken off the trip, probably for the best. RIP Jimmy, you legend.

As I said, there were two aims to the Tanzania trip: to climb Mount Kilimanjaro and to conduct a battlefield tour. What, I hear you ask, is a battlefield tour? Well battlefield tours, or 'bottlefield tours' as they sometimes get renamed, are a very good way of bluffing the head shed (basically anyone above me in rank, like the OC and Sergeant Major) into thinking that its soldiers are engaging in worthwhile educational training when in fact they are off on the piss. But seriously, as the name implies, a battlefield tour means visiting the site of some famous battle in the company of a suitable guide who explains what took place. It is a useful way of reminding the present generation of the sacrifices and hardships that their predecessors had to endure. Also, if you pick the right place, it can be an opportunity to study mistakes made and try to improve on them.

You may wonder quite what relevance the Battle of Waterloo and the charge of the Scots Greys has to fighting the Taliban in Helmand province, and I must admit that is not immediately clear, but what about fighting the Zulus in South Africa? That film, *Zulu*, has been much studied of late. It may be over 200 years since Rorkes Drift and the battles in Musa Qala but the set-up is the same: how do you hold out against overwhelming native opposition when you are stuck in the middle of nowhere? Answer: make sure you have plenty of ammo and keep shooting! The key thing to remember about battlefield tours is to make sure the guide is well briefed. They need to understand that what he or she has to do is ensure that while the morning is devoted to looking at maps and rooting about in bushes to find old trench positions, the afternoon is spent by the pool sampling the local delicacies, be they edible or drinkable.

So our battlefield tour was to Tanzania taking in Zanzibar. 'Hang on a minute,' I hear you cry. 'Tanzania? What battlefields are there in Tanzania?' Well the beauty of the British army is that its long history of Imperial service means that there are very few places on the planet where British soldiers did not take part in some sort of battle, and Tanzania is no exception. In fact, Tanzania was the scene of quite a significant series of battles in the First World War between the Germans who in those days had a colony based in much of present-day Tanzania, then known as Tanganyika, and the British who were based in Kenya.

However, do not let that little history lesson fool you. Neither I, nor indeed anybody one else on the expedition, had any real interest in early twentieth-century colonial warfare. Our overriding preoccupation was in getting a bronzy suntan and putting away a few Killi beers. Nevertheless, one challenge we could not avoid was climbing Mount Kilimanjaro. I know that lately, celebs like Chris Moyles have managed to drag themselves up it, but even so it is not something to be taken lightly. Pulmonary embolism is not a laughing matter and you would be foolish indeed to attempt an ascent without some form of rigorous physical training.

The trip to Tanzania itself was considerably better blessed then the pre-training, and to be honest I think the army got its pound of flesh out of us. Scaling Mount Kilimanjaro was every bit as difficult as it looks and the tales of the battles on the Rufiji River were genuinely exciting. We learned a great deal about Africa, life and ourselves. Certainly, I am quite confident that when we returned to Omagh we had far more to show for our exploits than merely a decent tan.

They say travel broadens the mind and I think I am living proof of that because I would not be where I am today if I had not responded to ideas and challenges that I met when away from home. Back in 1998, the QLR were asked to provide a number of companies in the dismounted role for one of the 'Medicine Man' exercises in Canada.

Now you might be familiar with the main training areas in the UK – places such as Salisbury Plain, Thetford in Norfolk, Otterburn in Northumberland and Catterick in North Yorkshire – and probably assume that that's all. In fact those areas are far too small. Modern weapons have much increased ranges and whilst those areas can cater for the very smallest of units like sections and platoons, if you I want to give divisions and brigades a proper workout you need to go to somewhere really big and spacious. To that end, the British army has for many years been sending out brigades and battle groups to the Canadian training area of Suffield in Alberta. This is an extraordinary piece of genuine prairie which has been set aside for military use since the Second World War. It is so desolate and featureless that individual trees are marked on the map. It is huge, larger than the county of Gloucestershire.

Each year, over the spring and summer when the weather can get very hot, we send out up to seven different sets of units and formations to take part in consecutive four-week training periods, each one known as Exercise Medicine Man and numbered one to seven.

Just to give you an idea of the extent of the area, during the first week of Medicine Man all the fighting elements of a brigade or battle group go to their own particular area and carry out their own live firing. They do this without interfering with each other or even hearing so much as a bang from anywhere else. This includes the artillery who are firing live rounds out to around 30 miles plus.

After the period of individual training the various units combine together to conduct brigade or battle group tactics using live rounds. This is the best and most realistic training available and trips to Canada are eagerly anticipated. My first visit there was slightly unusual in that we were a non-mechanised infantry battalion, which meant that we were moved around in trucks and had to spend all our time digging in.

I made the point earlier that how as a soldier one felt naked and vulnerable if caught above ground in broad daylight. This means that as an infantryman you get very good at digging yourself in to the ground. In fact when on operations the message is that unless you are moving, you are digging. You stop for ten minutes; you dig a shell scrape. You stop for a day; you build a sangar (fortification). You stop overnight, you dig a trench and sleeping bay with 18 inches of overhead protection provided by rammed earth. A properly constructed fire trench and sleeping bay can keep you alive even under direct bombardment, although what use you'd be afterwards is questionable. But ask the poor Toms on the Somme in 1916: the Germans had been bombarded for weeks in the underground bunkers yet as soon as the barrage stopped they were up and firing to deadly effect.

I am no Montgomery but I always remember in training it was drilled into me that the primary use of infantry is to hold ground. If you want to take control of a piece of real estate then the only real way of doing it is having blokes on their feet stood on it ready to defend it. An aircraft flying overhead cannot hold it, and frankly a tank cannot really do so, since it is relatively easy to sneak up on one and take it out. The only possible way of making sure that an area is secure is by having sufficient troops stationed on it and protecting the approaches.

Needless to say, exercising in Canada in the dismounted role, that is to say without the comfort of a warm armoured personnel carrier or tank in which to shelter from the weather, is not a pleasant experience. This was especially so in May when the ground and air was still cold from the retreating winter and the warmth of spring had not yet arrived. The exercise was a nightmare. We go somewhere, dig in. Then we move again and dig in. Then we move once more and dig in. We were like bloody moles and I got to hate the sight of my shovel which I used to cut my way in to the dry flinty soil of the prairie. Even worse, the weather was getting cold and lying in our trenches we were a source of warmth to all sorts of things that felt they might take shelter with us! Things like scorpions and, even worse, rattlesnakes.

One bit of light relief were the gophers: little prairie rats like chipmunks who were much better at digging holes than we were. In vain we tried to catch them but they were far too quick for us.

I mentioned that travel had affected me quite profoundly and it was on that Medicine Man exercise where I first saw something that subsequently changed my life. This was my first glimpse of a Warrior armoured vehicle. This is the standard infantry fighting vehicle for the British infantry and is very well thought of, not only in the British army but anywhere it has served. It packs a very big punch, with a 30mm Rarden Cannon and 7.62 Hughes chaingun. It is extremely fast and reliable across all sorts of terrain and is the perfect way to ride into battle. As I was toiling away digging my holes I watched them sweep around the battlefield, the commanders leaning nonchalantly in their turrets looking like Rommel leading the Afrika Corps. I knew then that that was the vehicle for me and when I returned from Canada, I volunteered to join the Duke of Wellington's who were Warrior-equipped and based in Osnabruck in Germany. Admittedly they were bloody Yorkshiremen, and I was a born and bred Lancastrian, but I was to be a lance corporal Warrior commander and that was worth being cast amongst the heathens.

There are four Warriors in a platoon. The platoon commander commands one and the other three are commanded by the lance corporal Warrior commanders. Their section commanders sit with their sections below. However, mindful of the stricture that the only way to hold land is to physically stand on it when the infantry assault a position, they do so on foot having dismounted from their Warriors. This leaves the four empty vehicles, or Zulu vehicles as they are usually referred to, with just the gunner, driver and Warrior commander in them. To control them, a Warrior sergeant remains behind in the command Warrior and looks after the Zulu vehicles. This does not mean he skulks off behind the nearest hill and has a quick fag break with the drivers while his mates are being shot to pieces on the position. After all, four Rarden Cannons and four Hughes chainguns are pretty heavy pieces of ordnance that you would want being used in your support if you are out and about being shot at. So the Warrior sergeant gets to a flank and tries to put down some suppressive fire, keeping the enemy's heads down and helping out his mates on foot; actually quite a responsible job.

You can imagine that to be able to spare a sergeant, three lance corporal commanders, four drivers and four gunners on top of the people to get out and actually do the fighting on the ground, a Warrior infantry battalion needs a lot more men than a battalion employed in other roles. This is why they are constantly advertising for people who want to join them in order to keep up their numbers. I was therefore gratefully received and joined the Dukes in 1999, but very shortly found myself selected to go back to Canada to become part of the winter repair team.

When units go over to Canada they don't take their vehicles with them. That would be an extremely expensive logistical exercise. Instead, vehicles are pre-positioned and as each battle group or brigade comes through, they take over the vehicles, use them and then hand them back before returning to the UK. You can imagine that the fleet gets a very hard use and needs a considerable amount of maintenance over the winter to ensure that they are up to spec by the time the exercise season starts the following spring. To do this, a large number of personnel are required to go out there to help the in-house teams maintain the vehicles and get them ready.

I was sent out for eight months over the Canadian winter, which taught me an entirely different meaning of the word cold. Temperatures of minus 20 mean that quite basic functions become very difficult; in fact positively dangerous. Having a pee, for example, when the wind chill factor is very high could result in the end of your dreams of procreation!

I saw a number of things there which were quite extraordinary. I was lucky enough to be given a place on another adventurous training exercise up in the far north. This meant travelling up a route that took in the frozen surface of the Mackenzie River. Whilst up there we played rugby on frozen lakes and in three foot of snow, which takes some doing. We also went dog sledging. That is one of those things which might look simple but is, in fact, fiendishly complicated. The dogs have a propensity, if they want to turn a corner, to do it at a right angle to the current direction of travel, and if you are not able to assist, they will simply pull the sledge over and deposit you in a snowdrift.

However, the most amazing experience was one night when we were all absolutely exhausted. We simply slept where we fell underneath the cold night sky. I remember waking up and being struck at how black the void above me was compared to the brilliance of the myriad of stars that pierced through it. I was stiff and very uncomfortable, and staring up at the huge vault above me made me chillier still, and then suddenly the sky lit up with a great green, blue and red curtain of light which flashed and shimmered across and then hung there like something out of sci-fi movie. I woke my buddies and for once they did not complain but lay, like me, silent and open-mouthed watching the extraordinary display above us. It was the Northern Lights, the Aurora Borealis. Despite its name, us northerners had seen nothing like it, coming as we did from places where the only lights at night were the sickly yellow carbide lamps on the streets. I am not religious but I did genuinely feel the presence of 'something' out there watching that awesome display.

You would have thought that was enough adventurous training, but in 2007 I was lucky enough to be included on another expedition, this time in totally the other direction: to the Grand Canyon. This was organised by the REME (Royal Electrical and Mechanical Engineers) fitters in the workshop. In similar vein to my African adventure this was another cynical attempt to hide a 'jolly' inside a supposedly serious physical challenge. The jolly was to be in Las Vegas and many might consider that a jolly in Las Vegas is a serious physical challenge in itself. In fact, I defy anybody who has gone there and taken full advantage of its possibilities to argue that it does not equate to a really strenuous period of hill-walking or some other intense physical activity. No doubt you want me to explain in detail what happened there but as those of you who have been can confirm, the watchword phrase is: 'What happens in Vegas, stays in Vegas' (except, of course, if you are Prince Harry!).

All I can say is, that after two nights in Vegas we moved to the Red Rock Canyon which is on the northern rim of the Grand Canyon to camp out and do some trail-hiking. The trip coincided with my thirtieth birthday and on that night we got completely blotto. The games and japes became increasingly bizarre and ended with us chasing wild turkeys through the cactus brush under beautiful sable skies lit by a brilliant full moon. When I awoke next morning I was shocked to find that it was 10 o'clock and I was completely alone apart from my mate Richie. Everybody else had high-tailed it back to Vegas, leaving us behind. That was one dawn I did not see.

I look back on those trips now with a mixture of emotions. There is a certain wistful envy of how carefree I was then and how I was able to enjoy what was offered to me and take full part in all the physical challenges, be they inside or outside the bedroom! There is also an amusement at how naive we all were: young lads brought up in the North of England and who in some cases had hardly travelled to the end of the road. Yet now we were visiting places which we had only seen before on television. Finally, in my case there is the satisfaction of knowing that, despite our attempts to get round the serious side of what it was we were doing, it nevertheless achieved its aim and all of us who went on these events came back firmer friends and comrades and ready to help each other out.

On one of my trips back to Selly Oak in 2011, I came across a guy called Rick Clem who had also lost both his legs. Rick and I had been in the QLR together. One look at Rick told me that he was not doing well and I spent some time trying to offer him support and encouragement. Much of that was by recalling the good times in Ireland and the fun and laughs we all had. In the army you seem to live and operate at a higher intensity than people in civilian life. After all, you not only work alongside these guys but frequently eat, sleep and shit alongside them as well. You get to know someone very well on operations and exercise and there is a real joy, almost a therapy, in sitting down and yarning, remembering what happened and the times when we all were scared or under stress or giving it large.

Rick has come back to me subsequently and told me how important it was to see me at that time, and how remembering all that was good and worthwhile in life had rekindled the will within himself to stay with it. That is what it is all about.

CHAPTER 5

KOSOVO
AND IRAQ

My first operational tour with the Dukes was in Kosovo in 2001. I was a Section 2IC in Alma Company back then and when they told us where we were going I must confess that I didn't have a clue where it was. It sounded quite exotic but when we got there it was anything but. It was like one huge pikey camp with all the population on the make. But compared to my first tour in Ireland it was very chilled out; no ECM (Electronic Counter Measures) to carry for a start and we worked in teams of four, which was great. Mainly it was foot patrols or patrols in snatch Land Rovers and in my team I was the only driver, which suited me, as I am a crap passenger and, as a dedicated and fanatical petrol-head, love driving. We would cruise around the capital, Pristina, and if me or the lads saw a dodgy car we would flash him over to a VCP (Vehicle Check Point).

One night on a foot patrol I spotted a car coming down the main strip and flagged it over. It was a Ford Escort Mk 5 RS2000 in mint condition. I chatted with the driver and he was sound. I had an Escort Si back in Germany; the guy must have noticed I liked the car but even I was shocked when he asked if I wanted to drive it! Now do I leave my three blokes stood on the side of the road and give this guy's car the beasting of its life down the main strip in Pristina, or do I say: 'Sorry mate, would love to but would get in a lot of trouble. Maybe next time!' It was a hard decision…!

I was sent with my team to guard a Serb church in Pristina. It was more of a big brick dome than the sort of church you see at home but it had a massive gold cross on the roof. There was nothing inside, just an 18 x 24 green army tent, but it was home for a few weeks. On the second week we got a message that a bus was coming through town and all the roads had to be blocked so it could go straight through. I got tasked to block two junctions. I did my appreciation, and troops to task, like they teach you at Brecon. I thought one guy at each junction and one at the church, all with radios, and me satelliting around all three – that would work fine. After we had been deployed for about half an hour I got a message from Company HQ over the radio asking me what the minimum manning at each location was. I told them it was meant to be two blokes. They told me to make it happen. I could not believe it. I radioed back that I didn't have enough men for two, only one, and ended the transmission with an emphatic 'OUT!' This means I do not expect a reply. But I got one; the operator at HQ came back on the net: 'MAKE IT HAPPEN!' He also finished with an even more climactic 'OUT!' I was now getting pretty pissed off and I was determined to have the last word. I got back on the net and yelled down the microphone: 'I CAN'T PULL MEN OUT OF MY ARSE!' I ended with the definitive and final 'OUT!' I knew that this would buy me a stiff talking-to, and it did. It also meant that me and the lads spent another week in the church. But it was worth it!

However, we did get a chance to put in some worthwhile patrolling. A few weeks later we were prowling round a woodmill when we came across a couple of cars. The mill was strangely empty but the occupants had obviously only recently departed. One of the cars was a brand spanking new, 5 Series Beamer. There was also an articulated truck nearby. I told the lads to check out the truck while I turned my attention to the Beamer. I tried the handle on the driver's side and to my amazement it was unlocked. I gently opened the door and peered in. A lovely heady aroma of leather hit my nostrils and without further hesitation I slipped in behind the wheel.

It was in immaculate condition, had only a couple of hundred miles on the clock, and was clearly somebody's pride and joy. In which case, why had he left it unlocked in a woodmill? I decided to open the glove compartment to see if I could find any clues to what sort of idiot would do that, and when I peered in I saw something gleaming under the courtesy light. It was a 9mm pistol. Ah, *that* sort of idiot! I gently closed the compartment and glanced keenly about me.

I told you that Kosovo was a sort of huge pikey camp and most of the population was tooled-up in some form or fashion, but to find such a weapon in such a car meant that we were in the vicinity of some pretty heavyweight dudes. Just then one of my blokes tapped on the window and told me to check out the truck. I did and was even more concerned to see that the container on the back held pallets of Marlboro Lights. We had obviously stumbled on a smugglers' den. I got the blokes into a defensive position surrounding the vehicles and called for a Royal Military Police team. They rolled up and gave the place a thorough search. Beside the pistol in the glove compartment they found a machine gun and more pistols in the boot. Frankly, we were lucky that whoever it was decided to leg it rather than take us on. Trying to cut off this sort of criminality was high on NATO and the UN's agenda so we got a nice pat on the back for our efforts, and the Beamer got impounded. No doubt some high ranking official took it on. Not me, worse luck.

In 2002, we were deployed from Osnabruck to
Barnsley TA Centre in Yorkshire, to act as cover for the
firemen's strike. The top brass thought that as the
Dukes were predominantly recruited from West
Yorkshire they would know their way around.
Unfortunately for me it was like being in a foreign
country. First we had to go to RAF Scampton in
Lincolnshire to train with the RAF Fire Service in how
to put out fires. If Lincolnshire is not the coldest and
bleakest county in England I would hate to go to the
one that is. It was freezing and squirting cold water
everywhere, and getting piss-wet through did not help.
We had to sleep in old oval huts that had been there
since the Second World War. We had to learn how to
use the by now infamous Green Goddess fire engines.
Fortunately for us and the good citizens of Barnsley we
never had to tackle any real emergencies. However we
did put out one fire. We were driving through town
and passed the fire station where striking firemen had
mounted a picket complete with the apparently
mandatory fire in an old oil drum filled with wood. As
we got close I said to the lads that this lot should know
better. They were on strike demanding more money on
a basic wage that was much more than mine and my
blokes', and we had been dragged away from our
homes to take their place. I told the driver to stop. I got
out, grabbed the hose and as I approached the group of
strikers, paid it out behind me. They had backed away
from the fire in concern at what I was about to do. I

stopped in front of the oil drum and shouted back to one of the lads:

'Water on!'

The reply came back.

'Water on.'

A great surge shot down the pipe and blasted out of the nozzle. I pointed it at the flames and the jet of water drenched the oil drum, putting the fire out immediately. Before the strikers could recover from their surprise I quickly retrieved the hose and jumped back in the wagon. We pissed ourselves laughing all the way back to Camp.

The year 2003 will stick in the minds of many people as the year of the 'Dodgy Dossier' and the UK government's involvement in the war in Iraq. To the military, the invasion and subsequent occupation of Iraq was known as Operation TELIC – TELIC 1 being the initial assault. I was still in Alma Company at the time as a Section 2IC in Osnabruck, and as a Warrior-equipped battalion we would have been expected to be deployed. But in fact the combat troops were provided by the Royal Marines and the Paras, with only 7 Armoured Brigade, the old Desert Rats, coming from Germany. We were in 12 Armoured Brigade who were not deploying, so we were all merely interested bystanders as the whole shebang got going. Then, with only four days to go before D Day, we were called to the gym for an announcement. It had been decided, obviously at the last bloody minute, that we be sent out to Kuwait to act as Prisoner of War (PoW) handlers. The next few days were the most hectic I can remember. You may recall that at the time much had been made of Saddam's weapons of mass destruction. Apparently he had shedloads of chemical and biological munitions at his disposal and as soon as we invaded, these would be showering down upon us. We therefore had to have all our Nuclear Biological and Chemical (NBC) kit renewed and all our drills and procedures practised. Running around in a NBC suit and a rubber gasmask is not much fun at the best of times but to be doing it in a desert heat was going to be a fucking nightmare! What was worse was that we were leaving all our nice safe armoured Warriors behind and deploying in Bedford trucks with nothing more than a canvas awning to keep out the bullets.

In a triumph of organisation from a standing start we actually made it out to Kuwait in time for the first border crossing. We rumbled forward, well to the rear, in our trucks. Blokes were sprawled everywhere in a chaos of bergens, kit and ammo boxes. Every time we stopped we had to pile out of the back and dig shell scrapes in case we got attacked. We arrived at the border where the Iraqis had built a huge earth bund to act as an obstacle. Obviously the engineers made short work of that and the armour poured in to take the country virtually without firing a shot. We set up our PoW camp not far from the border and almost immediately the Iraqi prisoners started arriving. They had no stomach for a fight and readily accepted the chance to get away from Saddam and the whole mess that was Iraq at that time. Sadly, an even more ghastly mess was to come but for the time being they were safe and well fed.

I reckon we did a pretty good job all-told and I was quite happy with where we were but, as always when things are going well, some bastard buggers it all up. After only a couple of days, a Yank battalion turned up to take over from us and we were told that we were moving further up north. In fact the lads were happy with this, as the prisoners were starting to piss us off. We moved up to Zubayr and took over some stripped-down Land Rovers. After the initial invasion it was very quiet out in the town; the people thought they were still under curfew. We had to tell them they could come out as and when they pleased – massive mistake! The streets became full of people night and day, all clapping and singing, rejoicing in their new-found freedom. It was a nightmare trying to get anywhere but the locals were happy and that was the main thing. After all, wasn't that the reason why we were there? We did some good work distributing water and giving medical aid. All in, it was a good tour for us with only one casualty, Jez Barkley, who got shot in the leg by a guy called Binos as he was cleaning his weapon!

That was not the end of my involvement in what has come to be one of the British army's less successful campaigns. In 2005, I went back to Iraq on OP TELIC 5. We were based in Basra, in the Shatt al-Arab Hotel. Never was a place more aptly named! This time we did have our Warriors with us. By now I had been promoted to full corporal and was a section commander and the platoon's Warrior commander. Our tour dates took in Christmas 2005 which was one of the weirdest I had ever had. Seeing somebody dressed as Father Christmas and snow scenes when it is 50 in the shade takes some getting used to.

Little exciting happened, although Basra was in the grips of a power struggle between the Shia and Sunni factions. Maqtada Al Sadr, who was the leader of the Shias and the Mahdi Army, was very hostile to us, and his mob mortared the hotel but luckily no one was hurt.

It was while on this tour that my life-long devotion to donkeys was able to take on a more positive stance. Whilst on patrol I came across a poor knock-kneed beast carrying huge sacks of cement. To my mind, having the awesome fire power of a Warrior at one's disposal is only any good if you can use it for worthwhile causes. This was just such a cause, so under the threat of our cannons the miserable owner of the donkey was forced to shoulder the bags of cement himself – much to everybody's amusement. He probably shot the donkey after we had gone but at least it would have died happy!

CHAPTER 6

AFGHANISTAN

In 2009, I went out to Afghanistan on Operation Herrick 10. I was 33 years old, a full corporal section commander at the peak of my military career and in love with a wonderful girl called Claire. How she and I met I will leave her to tell you but we had been going steady for about eight months when I deployed. Now here is the crazy thing: I volunteered to go. That is not the silliest part about it all. Not only need I not have been there but the company I deployed with should not even have been there either. I don't mean that our deployment was a mistake just that it was not done in the way that it should have been. Normally units deploy on operations as formed units. That is the whole point of the regimental system: we train together, live together, and work together. We build a bond so that when faced with death or serious injury we would rather go forward and face the enemy than risk letting down our friends and comrades.

However, the level of casualties the British army had been suffering in Afghanistan by 2009 had been so great that policy had changed. In short, forces had to be found to simply act as battle casualty replacements rather than reinforcing units. This was a policy that had not been adopted since the Second World War and is a testament to the level of casualties that the armed forces were sustaining.

Matters were made more difficult by the Afghan elections and the decision by the United States to deploy surge operations to try and roll back the Taliban and break their hold on Helmand Province. UK forces were to concentrate in Babaji. This was an area of central Helmand between Lashkar Gah and Gereshk. The area had previously been under insurgent control and was being used as a safe haven to plan, facilitate and state tax against the Afghan government. The operation to clear and subsequently hold Babaji was conducted under the banner of Operation Panchai Palang or Panthers Claw. Central Helmand was the vital ground for the insurgents and Panchai Palang had genuine regional effect in that it drew much of their capable leadership into one spot. Offensive operations on this scale against an agile, cunning and mercurial enemy as capable as the Taliban inevitably result in losses. The operations, coupled with an exponential increase in IED sophistication and preponderance (300% more than the previous summer), meant that the summer of 2009 was the UK's bloodiest to date in the campaign for Helmand Province. Task Force Helmand was under immense strain, such was the casualty toll. It was in this context the British army was compelled to generate battle casualty replacements on a grand scale, the like of which had not occurred since the Korean War. The focus of these was Burma Company group of 3 YORKS.

Burma Company was not held on notice of operations nor had it done any specific Afghanistan training, but because 3 YORKS had recently conducted pre-deployment training for Iraq, the company was rapidly force-generated for the task. The requirement had not been conceived at the start of the operation, and Burma Company deployed in the 17 days after the need had been conceived and formalised.

Because it was such a 'one off', the Commanding Officer called for volunteers. He felt that it would be unfair to force people to go on what was effectively an unofficial deployment. Many people ask me why I volunteered. I find this an odd question. I have already told you that I was a rifle section commander, at the peak of my physical and professional fitness. What else would I do but go to where I could put all that training and experience into practice in active combat? It was my job, and like anybody who likes his job, you want to do it in the most testing circumstances possible.

Once we were out in Afghanistan as a company we conducted an enhanced five-day training and acclimatisation package requiring us to learn new techniques and procedures. This was a difficult period made worse by the uncertainty and expectation of the high-level combat we were likely to face and, above all, the pressure of getting used to 50C heat when carrying full kit, body armour and weapons. After we completed the package we then split up. It was the company commander's wish that we did not split down any smaller than section size so that we would always be operating in an organised unit within our own cap badge.

Somebody told me that the United States has made it a rule that none of their forces will ever be commanded by anybody other than an American, and I think that's a very good rule. The fact is that even though we are all on the same side, units differ very much in the way they operate. The ethos, the atmosphere, the way they treat each other and how they get on are all different – if you've been brought up elsewhere, particularly in a northern unit, and then have to go and work for a bunch of moaning southerners, it can be difficult.

In order to write this I have referred back to my tour diary. My Officer Commanding (OC) Major Sam Humphries told me that it would be a good idea to keep one and I am bloody glad I did. If I had not, I am not sure I would be able to properly describe to you what operations in Afghanistan are like. I know this may be hard to believe but when I went out there I really had very little idea of what I and my section were going into. Sure, we had had briefings and as I have already described we had been on operations in Kosovo and Iraq but it simply did not compare to what we were about to experience. The sheer deadly intensity of operations in Afghanistan was something beyond my comprehension.

On 6 August 2009 we flew into Forward Operating Base (FOB) Nolay. We had been left hanging about in Camp Bastion for days and it was a bloody nightmare. There was nothing to do apart from watch TV and write blueys (forces aerogrammes) to friends and family. Blueys – they are a blessing and a curse. A blessing because they are free, easy to use and don't take up much space, but a curse because they are either way too small to encompass the amount you want to say or, more often, far too big. You come to the end of what you can say and yet acres of blue paper still lie before you like a blank homework sheet. Even with a big sprawling signature it will not hide the fact that, in what might be your last-ever missive to your loved ones, you can't think of anything to write.

Having quickly tired of blueys, all we did at Bastion was sit and watch the choppers land two or three times a day. In many cases they were met by ambulances and there was a mêlée of medics unloading the latest casualties and rushing them to the hospital. It was not a very encouraging sight.

Afghanistan is a dirty, shitty place where even if you stub your toe it is likely to become a surgical case, so not all of them were battle casualties but even so it was an unsettling experience.

At 18.30 hours, just after scoff, there was REPAT (Repatriation Ceremony). In my day we used to call them church services but the army has gone all 'PC' now and the mention of 'church' is deemed to be too overtly Christian. So, we now say goodbye to those of our mates who die in theatre by way of a REPAT. This one was for a lad in the REME who had been killed on 4 August 2009 whilst driving a Spartan, a tracked recovery vehicle that had hit an IED.

Standing there, listening to the words being spoken, brought it home to me that it is real out here. In Bastion you could be anywhere; it did not feel like being abroad or on operations but this gave me an inkling that I and my guys were heading into some deep shit. It put me in the mindset I needed to be in, listening to the service, and when the light gun fired a salute to the fallen, I nearly crapped myself.

We flew into Nolay at 23:30 – that is myself, Lance Corporal Roberts (section second in command) and Private Kemp. The rest of the section would fly out in a few days or when a bird was available. The flight started off OK. I sat in the dark watching the rear-door gunner going about her pre-checks (yes, *her*, pre-checks), checking her ammo and weapon before stretching out to lay on the deck looking down at the dark, featureless terrain below. There were a few lights denoting villages and homesteads but for the most part it was as black as the devil's arsehole, and like that orifice, at any moment something really awful could come out of it: a burst of tracer arcing up into the sky to smash through the floor, a rocket grenade or, horror of horrors, a ground-to-air missile. I was sat thinking about these possibilities and trying to keep down the underlying and increasing concern I had about what I was going into when, all of a sudden, the Chinook fired off a barrage of flares.

These are fitted as part of its defence against heat-seeking missiles. Being hotter than the aircraft they should decoy any incoming rocket away from its intended target. The sound of them blasting off from their dischargers was deafening, even over the throbbing 'wocca wocca' of the rotor blades. This was the second shock of the evening and this time I really did crap myself. The cabin lit up like Piccadilly Circus on New Year's Eve with an eyeball-cracking intensity of light. Fuck!

I don't know why, but I grabbed hold of my seat. God knows what I thought that would do if a SAM Seven suddenly joined us. For a moment I was more scared than I had ever been or ever want to be again. These bloody things are designed to take out supersonic aircraft, so even Stevie Wonder would be able to hit a lumbering giant like a Chinook. If that happened it was certain death. Even if you survived the blast, what was left would take on all the aerodynamic qualities of a breeze block. I could not run, hide or even fight back. I just had to sit there.

Fortunately, my period of exquisite terror did not last long. The door gunner must have noticed that this event had not been well received by her passengers. The smell probably gave us away. Anyway, she staggered over to assure us out that it was routine procedure, as the threat to the choppers was so high. I relaxed but I now had a further worry to contend with. If I was getting frights like this in future then clearly laundry was going to be an issue out here!

We touched down and I was met by a corporal in shorts, T-shirt and flip-flops, who welcomed me to Nolay with a smile and a handshake and said he was sure I was going to like it there. I have thought about this a lot since and I think he was actually being genuine! Anyway, I was shown to my bed space for the next three months and got my head down.

The following day we went on our first patrol – that is me, Robbo and Kemp. I was acting as a rifleman whilst Robbo and Kemp each carried a piece of ECM (Electronic Counter Measures) equipment. Our task was to go and find a command wire IED that had been located earlier in the morning. The call sign that found it had got split either side of the device so the commander cut the wire and extracted back to Camp. The Operations Room, exercising the infinite wisdom that comes with sitting in a comfy chair inside a secure

Above: On patrol in Northern Ireland in 1997.

Below left: Climbing Kilimanjaro in 1999.

Below right: Guarding that Serbian church in Kosovo in 2000.

Above: With my mate Richie (I was best man at his wedding) in the Grand Canyon in September 2006.

Below: Me, Robbo and Stu watching St Helens at Wembley in 2007.

Above: On one of my motorbike rides to Southport in 2008. *Inset*: My dad's BSA Gold Star and sidecar – one bike that definitely didn't have a happy ending.

Below: At a friend's wedding with Claire, not long after we met.

Above: At Camp Bastion just after we arrived there in July 2009.

Below: My guys (3 Yorks Section). *Back row*: Young, Kemp, Roberts, me, Hastie.
Front row: Moxon, 'Pogs', Bolton.

Above left: A blanket made for me by the volunteers at Headley Court. I asked them to put the motto onto the blanket and they sewed the whole T-shirt on – brilliant!

Above right: Wearing my ABF T-shirt with pride. They do a fantastic job working with injured soldiers and their families.

Below: Me with the amazing Sound of Guns – their music really helped me when I was in hospital.

Above: With Robbo at the medals parade in 2010. I was determined to walk onto the parade ground.

Below: In Thailand with Claire during our cruise.

Above: In Glencoe, Scotland, during the 'Numbumrun' in August 2010.

Below left: Meeting Prince Charles at the 2010 Millie awards.

Below right: At the Royal Hospital Chelsea's Founder's Day in May 2011.
At least Prince Harry kept his clothes on!

Above: In training for the Ultra 6 World Record Challenge in May 2013 – I will cycle alongside the runners for the duration of the Challenge.

Below: Back at home with Claire and William, November 2013. The boy is definitely growing...

shower, a wave of soldiers' paranoia ~aving me genuinely shivering with fear.

fortress with ice-cold cola on tap, reckoned that the patrol had found the IED before the enemy had a chance to get in place to set it off, and that as far as the Taliban were concerned it was still intact. If they were right, then there was a chance that if we were careful and suitably sneaky we might be able to catch the Taliban as they attempted to fire the device. Risk should be minimal, they reasoned, as the wire had been cut rendering the IED safe. Of course it was not them actually going down there to carry out this task. That was our job.

The plan was hastily hatched and we were assured that another call sign or one of the Sanger sentries had the wire under surveillance so nothing could happen to it without our knowing. These things always sound great in the briefing room but nearly always turn into a crock-of-shite once you are on the ground. This was no exception. We arrived to find both command wire and the device had gone. We went firm, that is got ourselves into a secure position, for about an hour; basically just to make us feel that all the hassle of coming out in the first place was worthwhile, then trudged back to Camp with the uncomfortable feeling that we had let an IED fall back into the Taliban's hands for use on another day.

Apart from that, it was good to get on the ground. The rest of the day was spent chilling and sorting out my kit. I had been impressed with young Kemp – I thought he might struggle on his first patrol but he had managed it well despite the fact that it was three in the afternoon and red hot. I also remembered that it was Claire's birthday the next day: another reason to be unhappy. Hopefully, the phones would be working so I could wish her a nice day. I was missing her far more than I thought I would and really looked forward to her letters. Unfortunately the mail system was not great, as the choppers were not flying non-fighting equipment.

Fortunately I was able to get on a phone and call her and we had one of those chats, you know, where you talk about all sorts of weird shit other than what you really want to say. She spent ages telling me about the snails in the fish tank which was, of course, exactly what I wanted to hear but we had a laugh and she had deliberately waited for my call before opening her card where I had inserted a few sweet nothings which she seemed to appreciate. I had actually gone a bit overboard on this one and sent some flowers as well but they had not yet arrived. I had the rest of the day free which meant I could get on with some much-needed laundry. One good part of life on operations like these is that you get to see a lot of films. Little of the avant garde art-house stuff makes its way to us; we are much more into escapism, as you might imagine. Some films are on a sort of permanent loop. *Days of Thunder* is one of them. I wonder if Tom Cruise knows he is so popular in Afghanistan.

After a couple of sleepless nights I moved my scratcher up on to the roof of the house; it was the best sleep so far. Heat is a killer; especially when you have to wear so much bloody kit. Sweat and grime, your groin stinking like a rotten fish supper and enough salt

on your forehead to pickle a cow's hide – that way of things out in Afghanistan. You can draining you of strength tonight, as the air and sweetens, and you lie under the stars you can feel yourself re-charge, the stiffness ebbs from your legs and arms and you awake genuinely refreshed. This was just as well, as we were sent out on another patrol to look for reported IEDs.

I suppose I should have been a bit more suspicious. I mean, if we were always going to be tipped off about these devices why did we need to fear them? This one was apparently buried at a road junction, so we approached it with great care but could see no sign of one.

Some village elders were having a meeting nearby: solemn, stern-looking old men who talked in low voices and sipped on their scalding mint tea. Little in Afghanistan seems to be any fun and this lot was looking suitably miserable. We assumed the presence of an IED in the middle of their village might be contributing to this, so we sent our Afghan interpreter over to see if they might tell him where it was. He didn't come back, so I went over to find him. This was my first foray into an Afghan village and I was a little nervous patrolling down the main drag. I was constantly buzzed by Afghans on sputtering motorbikes carrying huge sacks of something; heroin for all I knew. Any one of them could be a suicide bomber.

I suddenly realised how horribly vulnerable I was.

anywhere and anybody could prove to be fatal. All of us, no matter how well armed, equipped or good at our job, were vulnerable; we were like little kids let loose in a foundry. At any moment we could touch something that would blow us to Kingdom Come.

It was with difficulty that I fought down the urge to run away in shrieking panic. For one thing, that might itself prove fatal and for another I had a job to do. We could not simply stay in Camp and wait for the Taliban to dig us out. We had to try and take the battle to them, to dominate the ground, and to do that we needed Toms on their feet and they had to be led and looked after – which was where I came in.

But it had brought home to me the true awfulness of our predicament. We are trained to think that if we apply our drills correctly, keep alert and maintain good discipline we should avoid death or serious injury. The enemy would be deterred or prevented from attacking us. But out here that did not work. Anybody from a three-year-old toddler to a bent and crippled granny could be carrying a bomb and be happy to die exploding it next to you. Anywhere on the ground could be an IED placed where even their own children and pets could walk over them.

In the face of such implacable hostility, all those great soldierly qualities are as nothing. They will always be able to be that one ju ahead, and whether you lived or died was just a tter of luck and happenstance. You could be the mos efficient and switched-on soldier ever but you had just as much chance of ending up riddled with dockyard con ti as the rawest recruit.

After I had had my terrible epiphany I immediately felt a lot better. That may sound weird but there it is. I had just remembered a film I once saw. It was recommended to me by an officer. It was called *Twelve O'clock High* and starred Gregory Peck as a tough American airman sent to a bomber unit in Britain during the Second World War to sort it out. He gave a speech to them all when he arrived and part of it has always stuck with me:

'I don't have a lot of patience with this, "What are we fighting for?" stuff. We're in a war, a shooting war. We've got to fight. And some of us have got to die. I'm not trying to tell you not to be afraid. Fear is normal. But stop worrying about it and about yourselves. Stop making plans. Forget about going home. Consider yourselves already dead. Once you accept that idea, it won't be so tough.'

Consider yourself already dead. It sounds creepy but when you think about it, the idea makes perfect sense. That is what I did and, you know, it made me feel a lot better. Things were not so tough. Also it was good to get out on the ground; to be out on one's feet and get a feel for the surroundings. I went into the compound to see what was going on. The interpreter was there having an earnest conversation with a number of the elders. They sat in a circle legs crossed, and listened gravely to what was going on. I was suddenly struck by how familiar this scene was. On a Friday afternoon in Barnsley and Bradford, after weekly prayers, the old Asian men would gather at little bars and cafes where they would sit and gossip in the low, serious tones. With him being away so long I was expecting the interpreter to have a shedload of good intelligence but the useless prat had turned a bit native. He had found out nothing about the IED but had been discussing farming and the continuing poor harvests instead!

I should have been angry with him but I couldn't bring myself. The poor bastard had it bad enough as it was. Shunned by his own kind as a traitor and an apostate and regarded with suspicion by us, his was a lonely existence. We were out for three hours, so Robbo and Kemp who were in Bravo Team on over-watch had it very easy!

In early August we were warned off for a big operation in the Green Zone. The Green Zone: no, not a place where you get drunk before going out to talk to Jonathan Ross, or that place in Baghdad where it means a walled haven, somewhere safe. I can assure you that its Afghani equivalent was no such thing. It was situated in Helmand Province, and where Baghdad's green meant the opposite of red – i.e. green for safe – Helmand's simply refers to its colour. It actually is green, a stretch of fertile, cultivated ground along the Helmand River valley and it is not safe at all. The northern end, the Sangin district, is essentially insurgent territory from where the Taliban mount daily attacks on British troops. Of the more than 300 British military fatalities in Afghanistan, one-third died in Sangin. Its importance lies in Route 611 that runs between the lush Green Zone to the west and the drier but more heavily populated areas to the east. The strategy is to keep this road open so that supplies can get through.

The rest of the section was due to arrive just in time for the operation to start. My fire team was getting attached to the Company Sergeant Major's party in the Tactical Headquarters (TAC HQ) and Robbo's fire team with the Company commander. Not ideal; I wanted to work as a section on my own but in a major operation like this, designed to clear the Green Zone of all Taliban, we were bound to get that chance.

Before we deployed I phoned Claire – twice. Obviously I did not share with her my therapy of regarding myself as already dead. In fact, talking to her made me feel more alive than ever. Even just discussing the weather or her visit to the dentist cheered me up. It is a bit of a cliché but simple things do matter at times like these.

CHAPTER 7

FIGHTING THE TALIBAN

We are not completely at the mercy of IEDs in Afghanistan. We have a way of detecting them. It is a metal detector called a Valon. Valon operators are obviously very important but they need to be watched extremely closely. To be of any use they must make sure that they sweep the ground in front of them before they step on it. I know it sounds a 'no-brainer' but it is actually quite difficult to do. Nobody wants to be out for longer than necessary and if you stand around dawdling in somewhere like Helmand you can bet your arse wad that someone will take a shot at you. Accordingly the operators have a tendency to step and sweep rather than sweep and step. When we set off from Camp on the operation the route was already cleared, which was a good job, as Hastie, our Valon man, was moving his legs twice as fast as his Valon was moving. However, a brief, frank and forceful exchange of views soon put him right.

We got to Green 82, a compound that was going to be used as a Patrol Base (PB) for the Afghan National Army (ANA) and ourselves. It had already been cleared (or so we had been told) so we moved straight in and got some water on board. As I said, we were with the CSM TAC party as an IED team. Private Young was in a clip. In fact he was more than in a clip he was in a turbo clip. Carrying his ECM equipment plus pack and everything else down to G82 from Nolay, only about 600 metres, had reduced him to a sweaty sobbing blob: testament to the harshness of operations in Afghanistan. I left him to his misery. After all, it was his first patrol with the ECM and it was already hot, about 27°C even though it was only about 07:30. He would be OK; it's amazing the reserves of strength people can display when someone starts shooting at them!

The operation started well. We had successfully occupied our new PB and stores started to arrive so that we could fortify it. This is where the military is at its best. A wagon-load of barbed wire, corrugated iron sheets and sandbags arrive and the military engineers work like ants on speed, digging holes, moving earth and throwing up defences. You soon see how much this war is costing – no expense seems to be spared in producing the raw materials. It all poured in through the gate and we helped unload it while other sections were clearing down the canal nicknamed Route SPARTA that ran parallel to Route 611.

We were excited to learn that they had found some IEDs. There was a Yank bomb disposal squad with us. They looked as if they had just walked off the set of *The Hurt Locker* and were extremely cool. They borrowed my fire team as an escort and sauntered off down the road to sort out the devices, looking like the Magnificent Seven. I felt really chuffed for once. It all seemed to be going so well. Even though I was humping sandbags and breeze blocks in the PB like a bloody navvie, I did so with a spring in my step and a song in my heart. As was to be expected, it came over the radio that there would be a controlled explosion in Figures One (one minute).

Radio communication about bomb disposal has to be really terse and secretive. You should only have to say three things about it: that the team has arrived; that there will be a controlled explosion in Figures One; and that the team has left. That is it, no other information is given lest the bomb disposal people be compromised and attacked. These people are hard to find and to train, so their protection is paramount. This message therefore meant that the team had found the devices and were about to blow them up in a controlled explosion that would render the area safe. We carried on our labours now, reassured by the knowledge that the system was working fine, God was in his heaven and all was right with the world.

Thirty seconds later God was out of his heaven and was down on his face in the dirt digging in with his eyelids along with the rest of us. A brilliant flash was followed by a massive bang and a huge geyser of earth, debris and dust shot into the air from just inside the entrance to the PB, to then rain back down on us as we dived into whatever shelter we could find. From where I was now trying to wriggle into the loose dirt I could see a smoking crater where previously there had been firm, packed earth. Indeed, I had walked over the spot about ten times already that morning!

In the crater was the forklift truck that had been busy moving pallets about. It had clearly gone over a pressure plate IED and set it off. Amazingly the driver was OK, but shaken and stirred. The blast had blown off the front near-side wheel but quite miraculously it didn't go off when I and many others stood on it. The Yank disposal team hurried back looking a lot less glamorous. We gave them a hard stare, as they were supposed to have cleared this place. It was suggested that they might have another go and they duly obliged whilst we withdrew to a safe spot to observe. Over the next few hours they found five more IEDs around the PB. Their cool rating now gone, the disposal team had to work frantically to sort out the mess. Altogether they found thirty devices, command wire, command pull, trip wire and pressure plate. Mercifully no one was hurt but it was a sobering experience. Route SPARTA is about the length of three football pitches – so not long, but it harboured a positive infestation of IEDs. If the Taliban were capable of inserting that many in such a small area, what hope was there of finding them all and preventing their horrific consequences?

Elections – never really took much interest in them personally. Although someone once told me that Tony Blair holds the record for the number of wars begun during his watch as Prime Minister, to me, as a soldier, things seem to stay pretty much the same whoever is in government. However, when they decided to have an election in Afghanistan everybody got pretty excited. To be fair, they had not had one for years and when it was announced the Taliban swore they would do their best to disrupt it, so it was a very big deal as far as we were concerned. It was by now mid-August and we were warned off for a three-day patrol to the area of Robin where we were to take over a compound and use it to dominate the area and make it safe for the build up to the elections.

We left Camp for Robin at about 03:00hrs. First light is about 05:00 so we were hoping to be in place before that. Morning prayers at the Mosque are at 04:30, so locals were about but not too many. The move down was very slow due to the route and the weight of the kit we were carrying. My kit must have been easily about 70lbs. I was not only humping my own stuff but also carting a set of ladders like some jobbing window cleaner. I kept thinking that if we got a small arms contact I would be completely fucked. With what I was carrying on my back, if I lay down I was hardly able to get up again. Instead I would have thrashed around like a bloody tortoise, my legs and arms waving in the air. Unfortunately the route was bloody tortuous, with stream crossings and other obstacles to negotiate where we were forced to cover each other as we crossed them. This meant getting down into fire positions with all the strain of getting up again. Much of the ground we were yomping over was wet and muddy and with our heavy loads we sank into them like a herd of cows. It was a bloody hard slog and if God offered me my legs back on condition that I spent the rest of my life under the same conditions I would give it very serious thought before accepting!

When we got to the compound we found that there was a family living there and a well. Somebody tried the water and said that it was drinkable but I didn't trust it without a couple of Puri-tabs. These are one of the simplest but best inventions since sliced bread. Tiny tablets of bleach that you stick into water and stir. This immediately purifies it and makes it drinkable and in a broiling hot, shit-heap of a country like Afghanistan, that is a life-saver. You could virtually drink out of a slurry pit with them, they are that good. However some of the lads drank it straight from the well; fuck that shit! I think they all got worms!

The family was paid off and went on their way. Not a bad day's work for them. We started to make the place secure with three gun positions – that is, sites for the General Purpose Machine Gun (GPMG) or 'gimpy' for short. This is a rather humble name for a weapon that is anything but humble. A gimpy fires belts of 7.62 ammo at a rate of 1,000 rounds per minute out to a distance of 1,500 metres. With a muzzle velocity of about 300 feet per second that is a fuck of a lot of punch, and when you add tracer to the mix it is very potent indeed. The Taliban hate them because the tracer rounds set fire to the parched grass and vegetation, forcing them to either run or be cooked alive. We fortified the gun positions with sandbags and then set up some claymore mines. These are great bits of kit – basically a load of ball-bearings stuck on a slab of explosives. The idea is to place them in likely attack routes so that when the old Taliban come running up, you fire them and they end up looking like a piece of gruyere cheese: full of holes!

I was pleased that we had, at last, settled down with our new unit. I have already explained how we were a different cap badge, totally foreign to the rest of the battle group and I am sure it is difficult for someone who has not been brought up in the infantry regimental system to appreciate how awkward it can be to integrate in such a situation. I know we are all supposed to be on the same side but at times you could be forgiven for thinking otherwise. I was lucky, I was able to operate with my own section and most of them were Yorks. There was me, Moxon, Hastie, MO, and Lance

Corporal Roberts. In addition, from 2 Royal Regiment of Fusiliers (RRF), I had Fusiliers Bush and Connelly. The other Yorks lads – Young, Kemp and Bolton – had been put in other sections that were part of 2RRF but had kept their northern superiority in check and were getting on well with their new colleagues.

We started to carry out what we call framework operations. Once you move into an area, pacify it and apparently clear it of enemy and IEDs. But you can't then relax behind your defences and think that things will stay that way. Like a marriage, security of the ground has to be permanently worked at, with patrols, over-watch, and a constant alertness. For example, soon after we arrived we had to accompany a Tiger Team onto the ground. This term describes a combined patrol made up of Afghan National Army personnel with a couple of SAS troopers. Talk about from the sublime to the ridiculous! I bet those sorts of jobs are popular with the Hereford boys!

Otherwise we rotated between patrols and camp guard. When I was in Northern Ireland, camp guard was a bit of a bore, as the IRA were very unlikely to mount a direct attack on one of our bases. However, in Afghanistan that was certainly not the case. Camp guard duty was bloody important. The chance of the Taliban trying to attack was very real. Remember, the IRA had a healthy rational concern for their own safety. The Taliban on the other hand have absolutely none and are frequently prepared to do anything that may result in us sustaining casualties even though it means certain death to them. I know we in the West find this shocking but believe me when you see the conditions these guys live under you begin to understand.

Life in Afghanistan is a pretty shitty existence at the best of times, so the possibility, however tenuous, that you might actually end up being ravished for eternity by 76 beautiful virgins gagging for sex is understandably very tempting. One night, when Hastie was on stag, he thought he saw someone digging in the road way in front of him, so he put up a rocket flare and squeezed off some warning shots. I told him, next time fuck the illum and the warning shots. If someone is digging at midnight I don't think they are planting trees. Just shoot them. The civilians are under a curfew which is set at 21:00, so no one should be out on the road at all, let alone digging it up.

You have probably heard that tired old joke: do you want to lose two stone of ugly, unsightly fat? Then cut your leg off. Obviously with me, now, that has an odd resonance. Having three limbs amputated is a pretty drastic way to lose a pound or two but it has done wonders for my Body Mass Index. As they say it is an ill wind; however I do have to watch the weight, for obvious reasons. Getting me about the place is difficult enough as it is without me adding to it. Keeping to a set weight is not easy but I do have to laugh when I hear the wails and moans of all those who say that it is impossible to diet and that their shape is 'in their genes'.

This is manifest bollocks. For a start their shape is very much not within their jeans and for another I can guarantee that I could make sure that everybody who volunteered for the 'Andy Reid Fat Camp' would lose weight so rapidly that within a month they would have to block up the drainhole and run around in the shower to get wet.

What is my secret you ask? Simples: go and spend a month patrolling in Helmand in the summer in full fighting scales. The fat will boil off you like piss on a barbecue. We had hardly been there a month and already we were as lithe and skinny as a team of racing snakes. Even I, who can scoff for England, suddenly saw my 6-pack appearing in the mirror and everybody's faces became drawn and angular as stress and fear took their toll.

My delight and satisfaction at how well everything was going had already taken a knock. But it was soon to get a lot worse than that. One morning, towards the end of August, we were told to go and check out a mosque, as there were reports of Taliban being there, but when we got to it there was no one about. When we go on patrol we take with us a thing called an ICOM which is a radio receiver that lets us listen in to the Taliban as they chat to each other on their walkie-talkies. This suggested that a high-ranking Taliban leader was at a site known as Compound 5. So, naturally, we all dashed off there like terriers on a rat hunt to carry out a search, but surprise surprise he was nowhere to be seen. Now, I expect a lot of you reading this who have served in Northern Ireland will be looking at the text a bit sideways and muttering to yourselves: 'Bloody hell, what are they doing? This is a classic "Come on"!'

All I can say is that it was assessed that the Taliban were not that sophisticated, so we were genuinely expecting to find something. Well, find something we did, but as you have probably guessed, not what we wanted at all. After an hour or so's fruitless search of the neighbourhood it was assumed our quarry had eluded us and we were ordered back to the compound where another platoon was going to meet us and take over. We got there and started setting up, but on their way there they got hit by an IED and one guy lost his arm, so they went back to Nolay, the main FOB.

It was then decided that we would wait until last light and head back to Nolay. By this time we had been joined by the OC and the Company Tactical HQ, and would be moving as a platoon-sized patrol of three sections. I was to lead the rear section and Company HQ would be attached to my call sign. We set off at about 21:00, well spaced out and moving in single file along the route cleared for us by the Valon men. It was only about 2km back. Because of the IED earlier on, we headed west to the river and then followed that south. The fields are high and even in daylight you cannot see much, so at night we were just relying on our night vision monocles. These are image intensifiers; that is, they drag in whatever light there is and boost it so that you can see, but the view is a sort of ghostly green colour. You have probably seen such images on TV. We had only been going about 40 minutes when there was a sudden flash. Because these monocles are very sensitive to low levels of light any brightness causes them to flare up, temporarily blinding the user. The light burst was immediately followed by a massive bang that made the ears ring. The word came over the radio that Val, the platoon sergeant, had stepped on a pressure plate IED and was being tended by the rest of his section. We all went firm where we were and waited.

I would like to say that the next few moments were characterised by the calm and quiet efficiency with which we handled this crisis but I cannot, and you would not believe me if I did. This was shocking news to everybody on the patrol. Val was a very popular figure in the company but to make matters worse this happened as we were all strung out in the dark in some very dangerous country. Frankly, if we had all just thrown everything down and run off screaming into the night I don't think anyone would blame us. It was a very tense situation. However, I am proud to say that whilst there was shouting and fear and great concern, discipline, training and professionalism got us through. I had the platoon medic in my section and I realised that he had to go forward and help with tending the casualty. He could not move on his own, so I told my Valon guy, Fusilier Bush of 2RRF, to go first and clear a route. They set off.

Within less than a minute there was another terrible

flash and a blast, nearer now, that could be felt through the ground like the blow of a giant hammer. Poor Bush had stepped on an IED as well. I am not going to try and pretend anything other than that this nearly freaked me out. Things were rapidly falling to pieces. We froze, hardly daring to move lest we step on something as well. It took all my willpower to get up and get my guys going.

We needed a Helicopter Landing Site (HLS) to evacuate the casualties and the only suitable terrain was by the river. That meant we had to clear a route down to the riverbank, then cross over and clear the HLS itself. Getting a helicopter into a make-shift HLS at night is no easy matter. It is bad enough getting them onto a prepared HLS in the daytime. Afghanistan at night is almost completely dark. There are no street lights or other ambient sources of illumination to guide the pilots and they find it very difficult to gauge height and distance, even with night vision goggles. Anyway, we got it down and the two casualties taken on board. We later learned that the sergeant, Sergeant Valentine of 2 RRF, had lost both legs and an arm and died on the way to Bastion. Bush had also lost both legs but made it back to UK. Spookily enough, earlier that day Bush had told us that he would rather be dead than lose his limbs.

After the chopper had gone those of us left behind were not so much rattled as shaken to our very bootstraps. The OC was not going take any more risks and demanded that the Mortars put up enough illumination rounds so that we could see our way. If it meant making us a target for small arms fire, so be it. Getting shot seemed almost pleasurable compared to sharing the fates of our two colleagues. I will never forget that journey back. It was the most terrifying experience. Very cleverly the OC realised that the river would be our safest route. Not even the Taliban would be able to plant IEDs in its fast-flowing torrent. We waded through it up to our chests in the icy water. When we emerged we then had a short but very nerve-racking distance to cover to the Camp gates. The Valon men did a hero's job and any contact they picked up was carefully marked with a glowing Siloom, a sort of mini neon strip that lasts for several hours. Instructions as to which side of the Siloom to walk were carefully passed down by word of mouth. In such a slow and painstaking way we made our return. It took us three hours but seemed double that; it was a never-ending nightmare. We made it back without further incident and I have never been so relieved and happy to see a set of camp gates. There was a sombre mood in the base that night. We got back about 01:00 and I went straight to bed for a think and some sleep.

The two deaths of Sergeant Valentine and Fusilier Bush had a very profound effect upon me. For the first time in my army career, in my life even, I started to feel real fear and anxiety. The events of the past few days really got to me. It had also got to the lads and they were clearly even more rattled that I was. The trouble was, this IED threat struck to the very heart of our being. As I have said earlier, as a soldier, an infantryman, ground is as water is to a fish. It is the medium within which you work and you use it for protection and help you achieve your aim. You dig yourself into it, you use its folds and wrinkles to hide yourself and sneak up upon your enemy. The IED however turns the ground against you. All those bits that you want to use can now hide a device that can kill and maim. It was as if a playpen had been trimmed with razor blades. That within which you felt most secure was now somewhere where you were most vulnerable. In such times those seemingly trivial matters, like mail and welfare phones, became so much more important. I now really missed Claire and home. I was beginning to wonder if I would ever see either of them again.

A couple of nights later we had a service in the FOB for Sergeant Valentine. I wrote a few words for the RRF website. It was hard to do, but I felt I had to say something. It was a very emotional event. The Fusiliers had lost four people altogether and it was clear that they were all sorely missed. The Padre was great and struck just the right tone and he gave anyone who wanted an opportunity to speak. Surprisingly a number did. It was very moving, listening to blokes who are trained to be quiet and tight-lipped – and if they have to speak to do so briefly and tersely – express how they really felt. They say big boys don't cry. Let me tell you they do, like babies.

My anxieties whilst awake now started to trouble me when I was asleep. I awoke in a cold sweat thinking, why did I send Bush forward to clear a route and why did I give him extra kit to carry? His words – how he told me that if he lost any limbs he would rather be dead – kept running through my head. I had to sit down, calm down and rationalise the situation. He was the Valon man, that was his job and it meant that he had to carry the extra kit. In fact, overall he actually carried less than anyone else in total. It was not my best morning. To add to the fun we were due out today on our first patrol since the fatality.

We left Camp at 05:30 and for the first time ever I walked through the gates out onto the ground with a real sense of fear and foreboding. Never before had I felt like this. Not in Northern Ireland, in Kosovo or in Iraq. I was clearly not the only one who felt edgy. The Valon operators looked like a slo-mo of Tiger Woods putting for the Open. They were giving it about four sweeps to one step. This is another problem with IEDs. It slows you up. If you have to check minutely every bit of ground you are to step on, you can imagine that it takes a long time to travel any distance. Personally, I had no issues with them. They could take as long as they like as far as I was concerned. In fact, despite their precautions I was keeping my distance from them. I had learnt my lesson: if something goes bang I did not want to be a piece of it.

We moved down the Route 611 to some high ground

to give over-watch to another patrol. When we got there, I pushed the lads out to all-round defence and then sat down, had a minute and then called Robbo over and we talked about crap for a bit to lighten the mood. I walked around the lads and they seemed fine. We went back to Camp at about 08:20, just before it got warm, had some scoff and then got our heads down for a few hours. I woke later and tried to make a call but the phones were off again but then I got a letter, so that was good.

I started to fantasise about being home and waking up to a bright shiny morning, getting my leathers on and taking 'the beast' out for a spin. I think being on a big bike is about the best experience I can think of – apart from the obvious – and I can think of a few occasions when the obvious has not been anything like as good as a good burn on the tarmac. The teeth-tingling excitement as you twist in the power and feel the machine surge beneath you, the exhilaration as you swoop down upon a corner like a sparrow-hawk and the sheer joy as you thunder past motorcars as if they were standing still. I got goose bumps just thinking about it.

CHAPTER 8

LOSING MATES

At the end of August we were out again trying to ensure that the elections passed off peacefully and everybody got a chance to vote. The Taliban had threatened to kill everybody who did vote, so hats off to the Afghans who, by and large, did turn out. We went out to Green 82 and Valoned along a wall where IEDs had been located before. The Valon guy saw a command wire, so we pulled back and got into a safe area. Well, as safe as we could see, at any rate. I then went forward to have a look; it turned out to be some grass. A bit of a strange mistake but better to be safe than sorry! The rest of the patrol went OK but I heard over the radio about an IED in Sangin and an IDF (Indirect Fire Mortar) attack in Whiston, with one casualty at each. We got back to Camp at 09:00 for scoff and a lie down, as we were due out again at 15:00 hrs. This was to an area called 'Millionaires Row'. God knows why they call it that; it was a complete shit-hole. My team was on over-watch again whilst the platoon commander and the Tiger Team went into a compound to see some elders. I put the lads into all-round defence. We had been there about an hour, it was quiet, not many locals about.

I got a bit bored and was looking for something to interest me when I noticed a motorbike move from the north down past the front of the call sign and round to the south and into some dead ground (that is ground out of sight to you). Then the locals started coming out of their houses to walk away from that area. The hairs on the back of my neck began to prick and a funny, itchy feeling ran up and down my spine. I told the lads to be alert, and right on cue a sudden shot from a sniper cracked over our heads like steel popcorn to hit the dirt beside us, showering dust and debris everywhere. Adrenalin and training kicked in and we all dived into as best a fire position as we could and squeezed some lead back in the direction that we thought the attack was coming from. To be honest, locating a firing point is not easy but the rule is shoot first and ask questions afterwards. I managed to crawl over to it, heaved back on the cocking handle, pulled the butt into my shoulder and let rip with a cock-hardening burst of about 50 rounds into a tree-line that looked a likely candidate for our firing point.

Firing a GPMG is a life-changing experience, even on a range in the UK, but to do it in a hot contact is to move into combat heaven. With 4 BIT (that is four ordinary rounds to one tracer round) you can actually see the bullets in flight and, like using a jet washer on a dirty patio, you can literally hose an area with hot lead. The noise is deafening and you can see the rounds arcing into the target which erupts like a mini volcano. Some of the tracer ricochets off like fireflies whilst others set the tinder-dry vegetation alight. All the anger fear and frustration of the past weeks came bubbling out of me as I hit back at the dark fear that assailed us all.

Through the turmoil of smoke and dust we saw a guy moving about, so we fired a warning shot at him and he scuttled off. Then I spotted a guy with an AK47 jogging down a track. Again I fired off the GPMG at him but only got in a ranging burst before a stoppage brought matters to a halt. Frantically I heaved back on the cocking handle, opened the feed tray, cleared it, replaced the belt and was about to cut the bastard in two when I saw him stagger and fall. We stopped firing and watched the dust settle for what seemed like an eternity of silence. Then we got called back into Camp. We fairly danced back to the FOB. Fear and adrenalin in the doses we had imbibed is a heady brew and by now we were all buzzing like a chainsaw convention.

There is little to beat a good fire-fight to blow away the blues and we all felt like soldiers again. We had fought, and we had all survived. We were true warriors, tested in battle. When we got in we laughed and whooped like crazy men, and then a rather stony-faced company sergeant major told us to shut up, as he had some bad news. Indeed he had, Private Young, from our regiment, had been killed in an IED attack on FOB Whiston. Apparently he had been involved in clearing a route for his comrades and the people of Sangin and died on 20 August – Afghan Election Day. I hope that one day, when Afghanistan becomes a peaceful democracy, they will honour his name for the sacrifice he made to such an outcome.

After the excitement of our little battle this was a real kick in the family jewels. Somehow we had assumed, crazy and stupid as it seems now, that getting blown up and killed was something that happened to other people; to Fusiliers and Rifles, not to us Dukes. I know it sounds a bit arrogant, but there it is. Now it was our turn, one of us had copped it and we realised that we were just as vulnerable as everybody else was. It could happen to us. The lads did not take it well at all. A big prop that had shored up their confidence and nerve had been shown to be made of balsawood, and after the bravado of our fire-fight you could see the morale leaking out of them like sweat. I was devastated but I could not show it. I didn't know the lad but it was a big loss and I knew I had a big job on my hands getting my section through the next few days. You see, I was a lot older than my blokes. As I said, I was 33 when I went to Afghanistan. The next oldest bod in my section was

22, with the youngest being only 18. I was almost old enough to be their fathers (at least to some of them) and there was no doubt that many of them looked to me for that sort of guidance.

Fortunately, we were in Camp for a while and we could all lose ourselves in boring bits of personal admin. When you are out on patrol, carrying all your kit and weaponry, you are sweating cobs, and with all that is happening to you, sweat is not the only bodily substance you excrete into your combats, so that within a very short amount of time you begin to smell like a ferret's jockstrap. Now laundry (or dhobi as it is known in the army) is a touchy subject in Afghanistan. If you are based at Camp Bastion – or Slipper City as it was known by us out on the Front Line – you have a veritable horde of dhobi wallers, locals who wash your clothes and iron them to knife-sharp perfection within an afternoon. However, for us poor grunts out in Helmand Province there are no launderettes, not even a washing machine. In fact if you ever went there you would soon realise how ridiculous that image is. Besides, what true bloke knows how to operate a washing machine? Instead you have to adopt a very laborious procedure. You fill tubs with water, rinse your stinking garments, add soap powder and leave to soak for an hour. Then you come back, rinse again and hang out to dry. Not as smart but they smell better.

As you sit there, squeezing the crap out of your combat trousers, it is at such times that your home support becomes crucial. My calls to Claire were a Godsend. We did not discuss much, just a good chat about what we were going to do when I got home. I amused her by telling her about the food, which by the end of August was really starting to piss me off, because you couldn't tell what it was! It seemed to be something chewy served with either rice or noodles, each day and every day. We naturally began to wonder what the chewy stuff was. Whatever it was, it was getting very boring. Claire told me that she was round at her mum's helping to clean up for her auntie coming. Fortunately me and her dad get on great. I think he is very funny with a great sense of humour. I'd also phone my cousin Karl, and my little niece Grace sometimes answered. She makes me laugh; I couldn't wait to see her. Karl is the brother I never had, but I'm glad because when we were kids he was twice my size and would have killed me in a fight. I think he would now, if he could catch me! These contacts from home really did seem to recharge something within me and gee me up. The layoff also seemed to have helped the lads to cope with the loss of poor Young. The Fusiliers Padre sought me out to tell me that he would conduct a service in a few days. I was very touched but wondered how they would handle it.

I think that I should make the point that after the harrowing events that we and everybody else in the FOB had gone through we were not left to handle it alone. Obviously it is up to each individual to come to terms with what has happened and their fears and anxieties, but the system does try and help. One thing that they do which is very therapeutic is a thing called TRiM (Trauma Risk Management). This is a system that the army has taken on to try and keep us functioning after we have had the crap scared out of us. Volunteers, they can be of any rank, are trained to spot and assist those blokes who are involved in hairy moments and help them get over any hang-ups they might have. This is usually by meeting informally and allowing people to talk over what has happened, how they feel and what the incident has meant to them.

We had one after the terrible events of mid-August and I did find it very helpful. I know it sounds a bit 'touchy feely' and a lot of blokes don't take to it easily, but I for one am a fan. It was good to get stuff off my chest and I know the lads appreciated it and it did give them a lift, even though they were are still down about Private Young.

Towards the end of August, I started to develop a stiff neck. God knows why. I had to take some ibuprofen. On 23 August we had the service for Private Young. It went OK, the lads held up and Captain Denton came and said some words. As my ears are fucked, I could not hear a thing anybody was saying but it was good he was there and it really helped. I am not religious at all but I have to say that whether there is anybody listening to our prayers or not, just saying them does have some benefit.

By now the tour was beginning to drag. Three months

is not a long time. Stop what you are doing and think of the date three months before the day you are reading this – seems like yesterday, does it not? Well, when you are on operations in Helmand time does not fly quite so quickly. Late August meant that we were in that dangerous period. The buzz and excitement we all felt at the start of the tour had worn off but we still had two months or so to push, so there was no 'lift' of imminent home. Instead we just had to grit our teeth and work through it hoping against hope that we could make it through in one piece. Boredom was a big worry particularly during our days off patrol. Going out on patrol breaks the day up and makes time go faster but nobody wants to go on patrol in case they get their heads blown off. It was not a happy working environment. I am not a great reader but even I found solace in a book. I started one about climbing Everest; I had agreed to do the Three Peaks Challenge in the UK the next year, so I thought it would be interesting. The book made it clear that if anybody was reasonably fit, determined and had about £50k handy, they could get up Everest. The idea of being able to say that I had climbed the highest mountain in the world was attractive but at the price I might just stick with Snowdon.

The tedium has other consequences. One good one was that I was now getting used to hearing gunshots at night, so I didn't jump as much. I just opened my eyes then went back to sleep. But less welcome was that the blokes were starting to switch off. I was seriously pissed off when the CSM told me that one of my team had been caught sat down on stag, or sentry, duty. It was only an hour's stag duty, he had had plenty of rest and yet he decided to sit on his arse rather than keep an eye on his designated arc of observation. This was unacceptable for two reasons. One, it left the base vulnerable, and for another it made us, made me, look like a bunch of prize cunts. I went mental at him and told him that we had lost enough blokes when everyone was alert without him putting us all at any greater risk. As a punishment I told him to fill 50 sandbags. As we only had ten available I told him to fill them and then empty them and fill them again five times. His response suggested that he thought that this was pretty dumb and stupid. He was right but the punishment fitted the crime. As I made it clear to him, what he did was pretty dumb and stupid. I think it made him think twice about what he was doing. The other lads were no better. I told them to clean their weapons but when I came to inspect them they looked as if they had been left in a drain for five years. This was the last straw for me. I got them all together and we had a long one-way conversation about keeping up standards and not dropping their guard. I ended by saying that I was determined that none of us was going to become a casualty! I know; funny, isn't it?

Then on 26 August 2009 – a date I remember very well – we were woken up at 06:00 to be told that Fusilier Bush had passed away. I don't know why, but I did not feel sad, but relieved. I think it was because he'd told me he would rather be dead than have lost his limbs and, to be honest, at the time I felt the same. I had given it a lot of thought and had decided that I could handle losing an arm or even a leg. But to lose both legs, like he did, that was different, that would be a real challenge. I just hoped it didn't happen to me!

The tedium of Camp routine was suddenly broken at the end of August when we were warned off for a big operation to clear some compounds to the west of our location. This was a welcome initiative – we had been getting stale loafing about the FOB. To add to my morale I got about five letters that day from the family. It struck me that Claire and I had been together for ten months. It seemed like longer to be honest but I was really happy, and I comforted myself with the thought that at least I'll be home in November, when it would be our anniversary. That night we had a service for Fusilier Bush. These events were becoming rather frequent. I remember clearly praying that we did not have any more.

The operation was mounted from Camp Bastion. We flew up there at about 16:00hrs. We got there, waited around for a bit then I slipped off for some nice fresh tea and ice cream. You honestly do not appreciate how much we take for granted on a day-to-day basis. Good old 'builder's bottom' tea and ice cream; not an expensive meal but when you have not had any for so long it was like bloody ambrosia. I was not pleased to be hauled out of the cookhouse and told we were to practice heli drills. Heli drills? We had just got on and off a sodding helicopter that afternoon, practising drills was a bit pointless!

After that it was heads down, with reveille at 02:30. We awoke with a real sense of excitement and anticipation. We were going to swoop in on these compounds out of the morning sky like the Valkyrie scene in *Apocalypse Now*. We could imagine ourselves de-bussing out of the back of the Chinook into a 'hot' LZ (Landing Zone), firing as we went. There would be medals all round. We formed up beside the heli-pad waiting for our great whirring chariot to arrive. We waited and we waited. It was all rather quiet. Where was the familiar 'woca woca' of the Chinook? Eventually, after more than an hour, one did arrive. Rather less than enthusiastically we trooped up the rear ramp and strapped ourselves in. We waited for the belly-clenching lurch as the great machine lifted into the air. We waited and we waited, the rotors burning and turning, the noise deafening. We were still on the heli-pad. We looked at each other in dumb interrogation, then we looked at the helmeted RAF load master who stared back, inscrutable behind his dark visor. Finally he gave a thumbs up and we were off. The aircraft spiralled slowly skywards and levelled off and we waited for the spine-tingling surge as it soared away on its course, but instead it sank slowly back to the heli-pad and we were ordered off.

Disconsolately we trudged back to the waiting area

where we were informed that as there was no spare aircraft, the operation was cancelled. So that was that, no Ride of the Valkyries, no hot LZ, no bloody medals. We sloped off to the accommodation and watched trashy DVDs all day. Somebody once said that war is 90% boredom and 10% terror; too little terror in that estimate, to my mind.

There is a favourite army saying when you get buggered about: 'Get on the bus, get off the bus, get on the bus, get off the bus!' It sounds daft and is meant to, but it is amazing how it often it literally happens that way. This time was no different. After a day sat lounging about doing nothing and being told even less we were suddenly called on for orders and it was announced that the op was back on at the same time tomorrow. The army makes a 'big deal' about an idea it has called 'concurrent activity'. This is supposed to mean that when the bosses go off for a head shed or 'O' Group (Orders Group), us underlings are able to get on and get ready, so that by the time he comes back with the hot poop news we are all ready, straining at the leash, locked and loaded raring to go. It is a very good idea, but like most such aspirations it never works. We get told nothing, so when the boss does come back brimming with excitement at his new mission and expecting to find us all booted and spurred we are instead lounging about on our pits in our shreddies. This leads to a lot of shouting and yelling; people running round as if their hair was on fire, and while your training means you just about make it in time, you usually end up leaving your Mars Bars behind.

So at the appointed hour we were all ready to go, less our Mars Bars. We were a sizeable force and would need three aircraft to lift us. They duly arrived and again we trooped on board. This time my helicopter took off, and it was about a 30-minute flight to the drop-off. My leg was very soon in bits with pins and needles as my body armour dug into it, due to me being cramped up in the webbing seat. We landed so heavily – I reckon it was more a minor crash – in a field and we scrambled (in my case hobbled) off the back. The drill on these things is to get far enough away from the aircraft so that you are not swept up in the down-draught when the bloody thing takes off, then get down into a fire position in case it is that great morale booster – a hot LZ. Fortunately, once the three Chinooks had clattered away back to Bastion, all was quiet.

I took my pack off, set up the radio and got the lads to sort their kit out. It then came over the net that one of the wretched Chinooks had crash-landed somewhere en route back to base. Mercifully everybody was OK and had got out and then jumped on one of the other aircraft and gone home. We searched the compound as we had been ordered and it was all clear. Then we were told we had to go to the crash site. A Royal Engineer party was coming out to deny the crashed Chinook to the Taliban. To 'deny' is one of those posh words that people use when they don't want to say shit. In this case it meant blowing up the Chinook. Yes, you read that right. A very expensive and useful piece of kit, something that we are not overly supplied with, was going to be packed with explosives and blasted into metal confetti, rather than be recovered and repaired. Apparently it would need a low-loader, a mobile crane and lots of bods to recover it, and that was simply not possible in such a hostile area. So we ended up sat in the red hot sun covering the Engineers as they went about their business. At about three in the afternoon they were ready and we all got behind cover as the blaster shouted out his warning and pressed the tit on his detonation set. There was a flash of white then a bone-jarring boom and simultaneous tremor before the aircraft took to the air for the last time and broke up into a twisted jigsaw of pieces. We all cheered, God knows why. One less Chinook meant more walking for us. Then at about 17:30 three new Chinooks came to pick us up. As we flew back I reflected on the day: we had achieved fuck all and cost the tax payer about £2m.

CHAPTER 9

HANDJAR

September dawned and I got four parcels and some magazines that had been donated free by *Performance Bikes* magazine. It may not sound much, but I can tell you that it was like winning the Lottery (not that I have ever won the Lottery but I reckon if I had, I would be unlikely to feel much better than I did then). I was able to spend the day chilling and reading. We were on patrol the next day.

The mission was to be on over-watch. An IED had been found by the main road the day before. As we watched, an ANA (Afghan National Army) pick-up truck drove past the IED. We looked at each other in amazement. I radioed the incident back to base and suggested that they tell the ANA that this was not a good idea. However, about 30 minutes later they drove past it again. We watched them approach the spot where we knew the IED to be with a growing sense of impending disaster. It was like a film, when you know that something awful is about to happen. Some of the lads simply could not watch. I'm afraid I was fascinated, I could not take my eyes off of the battered old pickup truck as it lurched and bounced along the rutted tarmac. It bore down on its potential doom and as it passed, there was a sudden belch of smoke and dust that obscured the vehicle only for an instant, followed by the muted crump of the blast.

It was almost comical, like a scene from the Keystone Cops. However, the humour evaporated when they saw us and started shooting. Presumably they thought that *we* had set off the blast! Luckily none of our lads fired back and we managed to sort out the situation amicably. Even more fortunate was the fact that miraculously none of the Afghans were killed or even seriously injured.

We now only had two months to push. Days to do were getting few and it was very hard keeping morale and momentum going. It was becoming like that film *Groundhog Day* and everybody was starting to fray at the edges. One of the lads, a bit bigger and bolshier than most, began to throw his weight about and upset some of the younger and less assertive guys. I needed to get on top of this or it would eat away at their confidence and they wouldn't be concentrating on the job. The place was enough of a shithole, with the Taliban trying to make it a misery, without your own blokes chipping in as well. I had a word with the culprit and read him his horoscope. If he didn't change his ways I'd have to think of something interesting to keep him busy.

On 2 September, I don't know why, but I suddenly decided that I was going to buy myself a RC8-R KTM motorbike. It was a beautiful machine and to do it justice I had to get a Barry Sheene skid-lid as well. Together, me, the bike and my Barry Sheene helmet would look like the absolute nuts. It was extraordinary how much better I felt having made that decision. It cheered me up no end and I wandered about the base with a real thrill of anticipation as I savoured what was to come when I got home.

The next day the FSG (Fire Support Group) went out and drove over an IED. The vehicle was fucked but the only casualty was one lad who had a broken leg and nose. They were bloody lucky. I went out later and we had a bit of excitement: I noticed someone watching us. These 'dickers' as we called them were a bloody nuisance and a source of great danger, since they act as the Taliban's eyes and ears. I immediately sensed that his interest in us was more than mere curiosity. I stared back but he didn't take the hint, so to make my point more forcibly I decided to shoot him. Well, that is to say, I shot *at* him. Well not exactly at him but a few feet above his head. If I had shot him, I would have a bit of explaining to do if he turned out not to be a dicker but a very curious local. I always carried a few tracer rounds in the top of my magazine so that I could give a target indication by telling everybody to watch my tracer. When I fired at the bloke I could see the little orange flare zoom in a gentle arc to splat into the wall above him in a flurry of dust and debris. The dicker dived for cover and was not seen again. However, just then the ICOM – a radio that is set on the commercial walkie-talkie channels which the Taliban use for communication – spluttered into life. Over it came a sudden burst of Pashtun and our interpreter became quite agitated. He told us that whoever was speaking was saying that the IED is ready and they can see us on the high ground. We stopped and frantically scanned the ground immediately around us. There was another jabbering burst from the ICOM and we all looked anxiously at the interpreter.

'They are saying that it's not working, the battery is dead,' he told us. More probably our Electronic Counter Measures (ECM) kit was stopping it. I took the view that if where we were was exciting someone to activate a bomb, then it was probably a good idea to go some-where else, but you need to be wary. They know we can hear what they say, so they have often been known to give false information in the hope of luring us into a trap or an ambush. We pressed on and there was more chat on the radio. By the way the interpreter was rolling his eyes I could see this was more bad news.

'They are now saying that the sharp-shooter is ready,'

he hissed. We took cover, tingling with anticipation. Nothing happened. We got to our feet and walked on. The rest of the patrol was uneventful but we got back with a strange feeling of fulfilment. I know it sounds weird but I really enjoyed that patrol and I know the blokes did as well.

By now boredom was becoming such a threat that we would do anything to try and vary our routine. Someone drew up a sort of track within the camp perimeter and we began going for runs around the camp. This can be quite a dizzying experience, since you are essentially running round in circles, so you have to keep changing direction, but it helped. I realised that I had to get a routine going or I would go mad. By now we were patrolling every other day and as we had spare blokes, we could afford to drop a couple off each time. This gave me a bit of a headache. What was I to do? Stay in Camp, safe but bored, or go on every patrol, putting myself at risk but doing my job on the ground? It was a hard call.

What did I do? No brainer, stay in Camp of course! No, in fact just the opposite. You have to get out on the ground. Being sat in the FOB your mind wanders and I was starting to become homesick. I wanted to get astride that new bike of mine, and Claire was also constantly in my thoughts. I decided that whatever the risk, it was much better to keep busy. So I resolved to drop the lads off of patrol and go out as an ordinary bod. Well at least that was the plan, but you can't really just be an ordinary bod out there. There is always something you need to do or bring to the patrol commander's attention, which obviously gets up his nose. This was particularly the case with one of the first patrols I went on when I was supposed to be just a basic grunt.

It was now early September and the weather was getting quite cold, especially at night when the thermometer fairly fell through the floor. Our patrolling schedule became more intensive. We would go out in the early evening and would not return until the wee small hours of the morning. To make matters worse, we were sent off to Patrol Base Handjar for a week. This was even more out of the way than Nolay. There was not even a welfare phone, and Claire was very unhappy at not hearing from me for that length of time. I wasn't too happy about it either, but there it was. Handjar was supposed to be a bit like the Wild West. Quite often these reputations turn out to be a load of pap but in this case it was well deserved. On the second day we were there the Taliban put an IED on the back of a donkey, covered it with a load of hay and sent it trotting down a track towards us. Fortunately for us the hay fell off and the donkey stopped and started eating it. This was not so fortunate for the donkey. The Taliban, presumably pissed off that their donkey had let them down, blew it up. If it had got close it would have easily have taken somebody out. I got a photograph of the donkey's head lying on the side of the canal. As I said earlier, I have a bit of a soft spot for donkeys. After witnessing the cruel and cynical death of that poor animal my hatred of the Taliban grew much more intense.

The next day an IED went off in the wall about five metres from where my blokes were resting. Luckily nobody was hurt. I was in the Ops Room at the time and felt the blast. We were having a busy old time. The following day some Royal Engineers came down to fell some trees to clear fields of fire and we found two more IEDs. Bomb Disposal would not come down to blow them up, so the trees remained, which meant the sentry positions could not see the canal path. Handjar was proving one crazy place and I was not enjoying it at all. Matters became even less pleasant when I suddenly developed dysentery. I had to be back-loaded to Nolay, as I was spewing an evil yellow liquid out of both ends of my body. I know this sounds pretty dire, and was. I felt dreadful, but leaving Handjar made it somehow almost pleasant. I felt guilty at leaving the blokes behind but there was nothing I could do. Fortunately, they made it back – just. One got shot in the arm, a 'Blighty Wound' as they used to call it back in the trenches: serious enough to get you sent home but not serious enough to leave you permanently knackered. He was sent back to UK and now has a nice scar to impress the girls.

Once I recovered I was keen to get back out on the ground. It was now mid-September and Intelligence briefed us that the small arms threat had risen. As a result, when we deployed we did so well tooled-up: two LMGs and two GPMGs along with a sniper rifle, and that was just in my section. We were sent out to a compound where we were told there was a Taliban weapons stash. We were relying on info from a local. I would not trust a local to tell me the right time, let alone give me info on a weapons stash. Unsurprisingly we did not find anything apart from a pressure plate IED outside a door. We had a Royal Engineer with us who had some P4 explosives on him so I was expecting him to blow it up. But it was decided that we should wait for the official IED team to arrive. This meant standing around for hours like Figure Eleven targets. Sometimes I wondered whether the powers-that-be actually wanted us to get shot. Eventually they turned up, put P4 on it and blew it up. We could have done that hours ago and saved everybody a lot of wasted time.

Towards the end of September we got our date for departure – 17 October. On the same day we had another service for a soldier killed by an IED. The end was in touching distance. Could we hang on and make it out in one piece? All of us were desperate to get home; we were really getting fucked off now.

It was my birthday on 21 September but I had little to celebrate. The phones were not working so I couldn't phone Claire, and we were warned off for another stint in horrible Handjar. We went down there on the 24th and I was expecting the worst. I was sent out to patrol the canal bank, the one where the poor donkey bought it. It was very quiet. There were some shots fired but not near us. We went into a compound and there was a woman with kids who clearly did not want us in there. She told us that the Taliban wanted the compound to launch an attack but she and her family were not moving. Later, when I got back, I was told that my own departure had been put back until 22 October. The rest of the 3 YORKS party were to leave on 19 October to Camp Bastion. As long as I was home by 5 November, I didn't mind.

My memories of this period are hazy and intermittent. However one very important issue dominated everything. It was the growing desperation and gut-wrenching anxiety that we would all make it through those last few days until the plane home on one piece. We stayed in horrid Handjar until the 5th or 7th of October. It was a grim time. We knew that we were effectively on the front line and there was still no welfare phone, so I couldn't get through to Claire. She was also growing more and more worried that I wouldn't make it back, and being unable to speak to me made it worse. The campaign grumbled on. One day, the Commanding Officer came down and, as if laid on to entertain him, we had a threat of a mortar attack, but nothing happened. Then we were told that the Taliban were closing the road to the locals and if they used it they would be killed. Oddly enough, I was not overly concerned at that! Later, whilst dozing one afternoon, all hell broke loose with rapid firing and much shouting and yelling. Thinking we were about to be murdered in our beds we stumbled out, grabbing helmets, rifles and anything else to hand. We found that our ANA comrades had got spooked at something and had started shooting at anything that moved. One, near me, even fired off his RPG (Rocket Propelled Grenade). The trouble with these things is that due to the back-blast, the back end is almost as lethal as the front, so I was less than impressed! Once they had calmed down they realised there was nothing there, and looked a bit sheepish. We gave them our best 100-metre stare and went back to bed.

As the date of departure loomed nearer and our worry at making it back in one piece became more acute we began to get a bit impatient if we were sent out on operations that did not seem to have any aim other than just to be seen wandering around. We were sent on one foray, again by the infamous canal, where we located a possible IED. Before we could do anything about it the Taliban set it off by command pull and one of my blokes got hit in the eye with a bit of shrapnel. Everyone else was OK. The lad was flown back to the UK where they managed to save his eye, which was great news, but it was a pointless patrol.

We were sent back to Nolay on 5 October, much to everyone's relief. It seems a bit odd being pleased to be back in such a shithole, but Handjar was even worse, so there you are. It meant that I was able to phone Claire at last. She had been making plans for when I got back: a nice hotel and spa with lots of pampering and sleep. I decided that she didn't need to know about the superbike. It would be a nice surprise! I chatted to my cousin Karl as well. He was in good spirits and I couldn't wait to see him as well as Claire.

Talking of bikes, my detailed knowledge of them came in handy on one of the last patrols we did. We stopped a bloke on a motorbike and I was amazed to find that he had fitted a cigarette lighter to the handle bars, wired into the battery. I know, it is an old joke, so I pointed this out to the patrol commander. He was a bit dim and couldn't see why a cigarette lighter on a motorbike was so wacky. Clearly there was an ulterior motive, and so it proved. The Taliban use them to charge phones or batteries for IEDs. We questioned the biker closely but he was clean. Well not clean, because he smelled like shit, but he had nothing on him.

We were now packing non-essential kit ready for going home. The plane to Brize was so near I could almost smell it. I phoned Claire to tell her and she was very happy at how close it was to me coming home. I was excited now as well. I could hardly wait to be able to chill together with her; it'd be so good – and there was the bike as well. On 11 October the incoming unit advance party arrived. My lads were starting to lose interest in operations. All they could think of was flying to Bastion in six days. I had a big job on my hands to motivate them to keep their concentration going to the very last. I mean to say, it would be terrible to have come this far and then get hit. You would never forgive yourself!

CHAPTER 10

THE DAY THAT CHANGED EVERYTHING

I read the other day that you never know when you are having the time of your life. The writer's argument was that as you jog along you may think things are going OK; you might be a bit pissed off; but it is only at the end, as you are gasping for your last breath, that you can properly look back and say: 'Ah yes! That was the best of times.'

The writer's point was that this is one of life's tragedies because it means you have no chance to properly appreciate that you are living the dream at the time that you are doing so. That realisation only comes later, and by then it is too late. The opportunity to wring every last drop out of the moment is gone. It is a silly argument, but I know what they were getting at because I have had the opportunity of gasping my last. I have been able to look back and savour the highs and lows, and for me that period in the autumn of 2009 was about as good as it gets.

I was doing the job I loved amongst some great blokes. I was confronting the Queen's enemies and I was as fit as a butcher's dog. I was confident in myself and my job and I knew where I was heading. I had sorted out some plans for the future, I was in love with a great girl who I was just about to return to and I was going to buy myself the 'puppy's privates' of a motorbike that would have everybody drooling with envy. It really could not have got any better. Yet looking back at that period now, the overriding impression is that it was in another world, another time. It is as if I was someone else then and, of course, certainly in a physical sense, I was.

The day everything changed for me – ironically, and appropriately enough, 13 October – actually started really well. In some ways it was a minor triumph. The previous day the new Officer Commanding (OC) from the company taking over at Nolay had arrived with his command team. In any roulement (short period of duty) tour this is the first real sign that for you the war really was nearly over. Over the next few days more and more of your lot would be going and more and more of the new lot would be coming in. It is a very significant and exciting moment and it gives you the opportunity to pass on all the knowledge and information that you have built up over the weeks and months of your tour – the dodgy areas, the possible IED and ambush locations, safe routes, notable personalities and any other tips and suggestions that might keep them safe.

I had been selected to take the new OC, his Company Sergeant Major, his Intelligence NCOs and the Mortar Fire Controller on a familiarisation patrol. Why me, you ask? Well most of the section commanders had been sent back to Bastion prior to returning home, so I was the most senior left in Camp. I know what you are thinking but, believe me, I was happy to do it.

Our objective was to visit a few of the native Afghan compounds and to introduce them to all the village elders. We would be going out as two large sections with me in command of one and the platoon sergeant in command of the other. The platoon commander would be bimbling along with the new OC, giving him all the info on what was happening. I would be responsible for providing close protection to the recce party and making sure they didn't get themselves shot, while the platoon sergeant's section would do over-watch. Should be a doddle; I was actually looking forward to it. I had just ten days left of the tour; this would be a great way to say goodbye to the jolly Afghans.

We left at about 05:30, as the sun was coming up and I could feel the heat starting to warm the air and the breeze was like a hair-dryer on low. We were about 300 metres behind the other section, heading down to Route 611. We picked our way carefully along the track, with

Jamie Hastie, the Valon man, scanning the ground in front of us. I glanced around and was pleased to see that the boys had shaken themselves out. You could see that they were clearly in the zone and determined to give a good example to the newcomers. They were looking very tentative, as was to be expected, so our progress was slow.

I did a map check. The over-watch section was not heading for the right position so I called up the platoon commander on the radio. He agreed to go firm whilst they moved through my section onto the high ground. They did this slowly and carefully and started the climb up the dusty gradient to their correct location. Once there, settled into fire positions and ready to support us, I gave the signal for us to move off. I was going to pass in front of the over-watch section and move down into the valley where the compounds were that we wanted to check out. After a couple of hundred metres Hastie stopped. He turned and looked at me. The track ahead was blocked by some barbed wire next to a very steep drop. This was not an option. I looked for an alternative route further up and there was what looked like a footpath with a number of motorcycle tyre marks running through it. These looked pretty recent so I figured it should be safe. I pointed it out to Hastie who set off to clear a route along it. He was only about a metre in front of me, treading very carefully and swinging his Valon gently to and fro. I paced slowly and deliberately behind him. It is strange thinking back on it now; those were the last conscious steps I ever took on my own two feet.

I don't recall feeling that I had trod on anything. One moment I was stepping slowly and deliberately on the dusty ground, the next moment I was shot into the air, cartwheeling like a manic trampolinist. Then I crashed to the floor like a sack of cement and rolled onto my back. How did I feel, people always ask. Was I in agony? Actually no, but I knew something pretty awesome had happened to me. How can I describe it? Those of you who have played contact sports like rugby, or who ride things, will no doubt have experienced a really heavy collision. You run into a really solid prop forward or get tackled by some gorilla of a second-row. Or you get hurled off something to crash to the ground. Others of you less sporty may simply have done something stupid like run into a lamp-post or a door.

In all these cases you experience a major shock; it jars your whole being and you can literally feel your teeth rattle. There is no pain as such, just a bone-splintering concussion that leaves you numb and drives the breath from your body. I lay there just like that, my ears ringing with an all-consuming high-pitched whine, gasping for air. I was surprised and dazed but aware that something quite violent had just happened. I then became aware of a thick dust cloud that blocked out the light. As it fell, a thin layer of dirt and debris settled over my body. I managed to crane my neck downwards to see if I could see my legs; I could not. I looked towards my left hand

and was a bit disturbed to note that the middle finger was hanging off. I decided to punch the hand into a fist to hold it in. I looked over to my right arm; could not see that at all, either. I tried to reach my own first aid kit but then became aware of, rather than saw, people working on me. I could just about hear them shouting at me above the howling noise in my ears. I couldn't see who they were but I could tell that they were applying a tourniquet to the top of my right arm. Whoever it was slipped it over what I now know was a bloody stump and then tugged hard at it to stem the blood flow.

Only then did pain suddenly intrude. The tourniquet pinched the skin terribly and I screamed out in agony. I now know that it was Jamie Hastie who applied the tourniquet, despite being injured by the blast himself. He was yelling at me, assuring me that everything would be fine. As well as the ligature he also gave me a morphine shot.

When this kicked in, life became a whole lot better, but then a horrible thought intruded. I turned to Jamie and asked him a question you would only ask a special friend: could he check that my wedding tackle was all in place. At that moment that was all that was important to me. Was my 'old man' still where it should be? He assured me that it was and I felt a genuine flood of relief. That really was all that was troubling me at that particular moment. The section, I knew, would look after themselves. For me, the war was finished. I could relax and let the system take over, and I did. In fact I passed out. I later learnt that they decided to evacuate me back to Nolay on a Jackal armoured vehicle. As we had already cleared the route out to where I was, they could risk it rather than wait for a helicopter. Besides, its downdraught may have set off other devices in the vicinity. So I had to lie in the Afghan dirt waiting till they could drive out and pick me up.

I must have drifted off because I remember jerking back to consciousness as I was being loaded on to the Jackal. On TV programmes like *Casualty* you often see slick paramedics sliding stretchers smoothly into the back of an ambulance before being whisked off with lights flashing and sirens blaring. This was not my recollection. I had to be heaved up into the vehicle like a plank of wood and then driven back to Camp bumping and swaying over every rut and pothole. Somebody was beside me, reassuring me that everything was fine and that I would be on *Strictly Come Dancing* next year. Sounds stupid shit but I have to say I did find it helpful.

Eventually we ground to a halt in Nolay and I was hauled off and taken into the Med tent. The medic yelled in my ear that a heli was in-bound and due in six minutes. I lay back reassured that all was going well. But then I overheard him talking to his mates. He obviously assumed I was out of it because he made no attempt to lower his voice. Apparently there was no med team on board the in-bound aircraft and so he had ordered another one because he didn't think I would survive back to Bastion without proper medical supervision on the way. This did not sound so good. Then he announced that a US helicopter with a MERT on board was only ten minutes away and they had agreed to pick me up. MERT stands for Medical Emergency Resuscitation Team – that sounded like exactly what I needed.

I was taken out of the Med tent and put in another tent by the heli-pad. They covered me with a sheet to keep the worst of the shit kicked up by the helicopter downdraught off me and then left me there. Suddenly, Hastie came into view. I was not aware of it but he had copped a piece of the shrapnel from my bomb, up where the sun don't shine, so was in some pain himself and would accompany me back to Bastion. Many people who know nothing about operations in Afghanistan have since asked me whether I was angry at him for not detecting the device that blew me up. Not a bit of it. In fact he later received the Queen's Commendation for his efforts in saving my life. Never was an award more truly deserved. The fact that his Valon did not locate the IED was certainly not his fault. The Valon operates over a wide range of frequencies that are labelled 1 to 10. On the day, his Valon was set to 3 to 4 but the Taliban are wise to this, so use as much non-metallic components in their IEDs as possible. This means that the Valon simply cannot pick them up. This is the great problem with these weapons; whether you get hit or not is simply a matter of luck. You can be the best, most careful soldier in the army but if you step in the wrong place you are a 'goner', and there's jack shit you can do about it.

I tried to talk to him but the morphine had by now penetrated deeper into my brain and I started to talk gibberish and lapsed in and out of consciousness. I lay there, staring up at the green canvas and the aluminium ridge poles of the tented roof and I remember wondering whether it would stand the downdraught of the incoming aircraft. That would be all I needed after being blown to shit by an IED: getting tossed across the compound like a piece of tumbleweed. In the military medicine world the watchword is the 'Golden Hour'. If you can get the casualty to a proper surgical facility within the first hour after injury you have a good chance of saving him. Fortunately for me, the incoming MERT aircraft would get me there in good time. Well, at least that was the plan.

What I had not counted on was them trying to terminate my chances en route! I have no memory of being loaded onto the aircraft but I have a very vivid recollection of being asked if I was OK and me replying that I was thirsty, could I have some water. The medic duly obliged by pulling out his own water bottle and undid the top. He then tipped it towards my parched lips. However, I was lying down and we were in a helicopter zooming across the Afghan countryside. The inevitable happened and he poured almost the entire contents of the bottle over my mouth and nose, making me cough and splutter for breath. Bloody marvellous! I manage to survive a bomb only to be drowned by my supposed saviours!

It was there and then that I made a solemn pledge to myself: I was not going to put up with any shit from anybody any more. I had paid my dues, I had expended three limbs to the cause, and now I owed nothing in the way of deference or obligation. If I was angry or pissed off then it would be for the other person to get over it. I was not going to be the one to make any accommodations. You think about it: a bloke in a wheelchair missing three limbs has every right to be spitting angry, and to expect him to be anything else is a bloody big 'ask'. The fact that they do not bite your head off when you speak to them is a great testament to their ability to adapt – but don't take it for granted.

That was it, my last memories of Afghanistan, a sudden and intense rage. I only had ten sodding days left and I would have been safely home, all my limbs intact. But no, I had to go and step on a bloody landmine like a stupid tit. I had let everybody down, especially myself. What would Claire say? Bang went the bomb and with it bang went my lovely bike. What a pisser!

CHAPTER 11

KARL'S STORY

I am Karl, Andy's cousin. A number of people have told me that I am the brother that Andy never had. I am not sure what that means but we grew up together and I suppose we have always been very close; certainly good mates. I remember hearing about his injury as if it was only this morning. I received a call from my dad and I knew at once that something was wrong; I could hear it in his voice. As he started to cry, my first thought was that it was Mum, but then he managed to blurt out:

'It's Andrew, he's been hurt'.

That was enough. I sort of panicked and started rambling down the phone at him, asking how bad his injuries were but Dad couldn't stop crying. At this point it suddenly dawned on me that Andy may be dead. I put the question there and then. Thankfully Dad was able to tell me that he was still alive but that he may die soon. Nobody yet knew how serious he was.

I listened in a daze as Dad went on to tell me that Andrew had been blown up, and that he had lost his both legs and broken his arm. I asked if there was any more damage but he didn't know. I suspected that he was keeping something from me, but I was so upset that I was unable to press him on the point but, in any case, he was too upset to tell me.

He rang off. I then threw the phone away and screamed. I was so angry: angry at the Government, angry at the war, even angry at Dad for bringing me the terrible news. I just could not believe what I was being told. I decided that I had to get to Claire. I had to find out if she knew and if she did, to try and comfort her, though with my head so in bits, God knows what help I would be. My wife (yet another Clare) came home from work. She already knew, as Dad had phoned her trying to get to me. She was devastated but amazingly calm. It is funny how women are often better in these situations than blokes.

I called Andy's dad to see if I could find out any more information. He was very much in control; much more than I was in fact and he told me to stop crying. He said that Andy would be OK, that he is a stubborn bastard and this will not stop him. He invited me over to their house and I went and found all his close family were there. They told me that the army had sent a driver to pick up his parents and Claire, and take them all down to Selly Oak. Apparently Andy had been stabilised but was in a coma and was on a medical flight back home from Bastion at that very moment.

The next 24 hours went by in a blur but I can recall them vividly to this day. Back in St Helens we were getting regular reports from Claire and Andy's mum and dad. It was they who told us that Andy had been on a morning patrol and that he had trodden on an IED. They confirmed that he had indeed lost both of his legs and his right arm. I was deeply shocked. Andy had always been a very physical guy. How was he going to cope with virtually all his limbs missing?

The next day my wife suggested that we both go to Birmingham to support Claire and try to help her take her mind off things. Whilst we were thinking this through we got a call from Andy's dad to say that Andy was up for a visit, and if we wanted to, he would like to see us. It was the hardest decision in the world. I admit I have never been so scared as I was on that drive to the Selly Oak hospital. I simply had no idea what to expect. We were met by the family liaison officer, a Sergeant Major Ian Lister. He was incredible; he led Clare and me to the military ward where we met Claire and Andy's parents in the waiting room. Everyone was pretty emotional and in a state of shock, it still had not sunk in what had happened to Andy.

Ian led us to the ward and before going in he stopped, grabbed me by the arm, looked me straight in the eye and whispered: 'Don't cry, don't pass out and above all don't throw up!'

I nodded dumbly. Shit! How bad was he? What have they not told me about him? What am I going to see that I do not already know? I mean, was he horribly burnt, disfigured? As we walked along the ward I focused on getting to Andy's bed, which as it happens was at the very end. We could see bed after bed of young soldiers, once fit men, damaged beyond recognition. It was heartbreaking.

Andy was on the last bed. As soon as I saw him I had to literally choke back the tears. For a start he was so skinny. His skin was tanned from almost six months in the blazing Afghan sun and his hair was like a Seventies Afro, but it was his eyes that unnerved me the most. He has blue eyes but these were like chips of sapphire; completely piercing due to the morphine. I could see that he recognised me at once. To my amazement his face broke into a beaming smile.

'All right mate?' His voice was a hoarse whisper.

I laughed in utter relief. I could see that it was him, my best mate; still the same after 30-odd years... thank GOD! However, it was clear that he was in a mess. His right arm looked as though someone had hacked it off just above the elbow with a blunt axe. He tried his best to hide the rawness of it – typical Andy, always thinking of others before himself. His legs were covered but you could see that there were blank spaces where his feet should have been. It really was hard not to cry. We chatted away, talking total shit until it was time to go. My wife was incredible. She just sat and talked to him, telling him she was glad he was home safe and that Grace, our daughter, missed him and reassuring him that everything would be OK.

Andy's Claire was on the opposite side of the bed. How she had held it together over the first few days I have no idea; I have so much respect for her. It reassured me. I knew he was going to be fine because he had found a girl who loves him for himself and not for the materialistic bollocks that many girls go for. I know many that would have been off like an escaping greyhound as soon as they had heard that their boyfriend had been so badly injured, but not Claire.

Andy commented on the jacket I was wearing, a Barbour bikers' jacket that I had only recently bought. He took the piss, asking where the belt was. I told him that I didn't like the belt, and he teased me, accusing me of being too fat to wear it. I knew at that moment he was definitely going to be fine. When it came time for us to go I tried to reassure him and told him not to worry about anything other than getting better, staying strong and focusing on coming home. He saw that something was wrong and he asked me what was up? I told him I wanted to hug him, but I didn't know where to touch him because of the wires from the life support. He told me not to be a prick and leant forward and wrapped his one-and-a-half arms around me as best he could. I kissed his head and told him again that it was all going to be

OK. He fell back on his pillows, winked and it was time to go.

When we got back to the hotel, it all just came out. I don't mind admitting it, I cried like a baby; I was so hurt, so upset for him. I love Andy like a brother, in fact more so because he is my closest friend. It has been that way since we were kids. He never had any brothers, only sisters, so I guess that is why we are so close. And it killed me to see him so hurt and damaged. To be honest, I didn't want to go back the next day, the pain of seeing him in that state was so raw. Clare comforted me as best she could, although I could see she was equally upset. We both fell silent but we knew what each other was thinking. How was he going to live, or cope and have a normal life? But we both agreed: nothing stops him, and these injuries will not hold him back, if anything they will push him on.

The next day we went back for lunch. My Clare, being the perfect mother she is, decided that home comforts were needed. She popped into Yo Sushi and the Clinique counter at Selfridges on the way. We were determined to spoil him. She thought he looked as if he needed some Clinique moisturiser and he was grateful for it! It was great fun buying him girly make-up items. The visits became more regular. I wanted to be available at any time for both Claire and Andy. Claire needed the support and a break from her constant vigil, and Andy needed some blokey banter and reassurance that everything would be fine.

We took the decision to tell our daughter Grace about it two weeks after Andy was home. By now he was scootering about in his wheelchair, so he was comfortable enough to see her and take the questions that she would undoubtedly ask. For us, it was the hardest decision as a parent we had had to make. How do you tell a 5-year-old that her uncle had been blown up? It is not something you ever think you will do, but we had to. Grace's first response was to ask whether he could still dance. Andy has a great relationship with Grace. He loves her to bits and it is the same in return. We explained what had happened and reassured her that it will never happen to her. She immediately said that she wanted to see him and we took her down on a Sunday.

Andy met us in the canteen and his face lit up when he saw her. I could see that she was taken aback. Andy scooped her up and sat her on his knee and she just buried her head into his chest. It was quite an emotional moment. He told her that he would be OK and made her feel comfortable. Then they went for a little ride on his chair and she was fine, she took it all in her stride and I think Andy was equally as pleased to see her as she was to see him after so long.

Over time you come to accept what has happened. Well perhaps not accept but you see that Andy is living his life to the best of his abilities. He is heavily involved with charity work, and he has set up a lovely home with Claire at his side, and whilst his body is radically different to what it was, inside he is still the same bloke.

147

He is still the same Andy who I have known and loved all my life. I know that he has coped wonderfully but I am not sure the rest of us have. I have found it very hard to come to terms with. Counselling has helped but there is not a day goes by that I don't think about him or worry about him, even though I know that he and Claire will live very fulfilled lives together. I can't help myself. I love him as though he is my younger brother and I will always try to look after him, even it does get on his tits...

CHAPTER 12

CLAIRE'S STORY

The first time I met Andy Reid was on 27 November 2008. We had been chatting to each other on Facebook and we had arranged to meet in a pub called the Wheatsheaf where I used to work on a Friday night. I worked with his sister, and her 30th birthday was approaching so he messaged me to discuss what we could do for her. He was in Canada at the time and was missing home so I assumed that the reason he was messaging me every day was because he was homesick and because he had time to spare. I found talking to him really interesting. He had many a funny story to tell, and it was so different to my mundane day-to-day life working in an accounts department.

We arranged to meet on this particular night and to

be perfectly honest I was reluctant to go. I knew that he was going to be out with a friend beforehand and that they were going to a beer festival. I was concerned that he would turn up drunk, but my best friend Emma encouraged me to go. She and all my friends were all intrigued about this 'army man' who I had been talking so much about. So I got myself ready and drove to the Wheatsheaf. He was not there when I arrived but fortunately I knew the place well so I just sat and chatted with the locals for a while. Then he came in through the door.

He was tall, dark and handsome, even more so than in his pictures, but my suspicions were proved correct. He was drunk! However, it didn't take much persuasion for me to leave my car and get drunk along with him and his mate. Before I knew it, I had several double vodkas down me and had sent Emma a few texts about him being 'really fit!' Then we went dancing in the local nightclub. At the end of the night we said our goodbyes. I thought nothing would come of it and I would not see him again: he was in the army and he was away all the time. He told me he would text me but I didn't believe him. I thought it was just something you say when you say goodbye. I was mistaken. The next morning I had a text from him asking how my head was and just random chit-chat. I was really chuffed; I thought he must like me! He then texted me to go on a date with him, and of course I said yes straight away. In fact we didn't go out; instead he cooked me a three-course meal and bought in my favourite wine. I was very impressed. He was so considerate and he had obviously gone to a lot of effort. After that he went back to Camp and was away all through the week but when he came home on a Friday we would see each other as much as possible. He went to extreme lengths to come home on a weekend to see me (well that's what I hoped) by borrowing his Nan's car which is 25 years old and hasn't done many long journeys in its time... in the snow!

He invited me to his Christmas 'Mess do' and I drove down to Warminster where he was based. It was then that we decided that we would be a couple officially. We had such a great time at the 'do' and managed to lock ourselves out of the block where Andy's room was. He had to climb through the laundry window to let us in... I kept panicking that he was going to get into trouble.

On the day, or I should say at the moment, I was told that Andy was going to Afghanistan in four days' time it was as if I had been punched in the stomach. I felt physically sick. I had watched the news and I was aware of the dangers that he would face. It never occurred to me that he would get injured – you never hear anything about the men and women who have been hurt, you only hear about the people who have died.

During the entire time he was away I wrote to him every day. Then every couple of days I sent him boxes of goodies. I knew that he wouldn't want half of it but I was so keen to let him know that I was thinking about him. He would phone me as often as he could but some days I didn't get a call. I knew that this meant that the lines had been closed down because a soldier had been killed. Andy had told me that if anything were to happen to him I would be told straight away. So no news was good news, at least for me!

Then came that dreadful day in October 2009 when Andy's and my luck ran out, and no news became bad news. Initially I was in denial. I simply could not process the information I had been told. How could someone still live after losing both legs and an arm? How much pain was he in? I had visions of what I thought might have happened but I could not picture his face. I could not bear to be around people and didn't want to be hugged or even cry because I just could not take it all in. Andy's family, despite being totally devastated themselves, tried to get me to stay over at their house that night to make sure I was OK.

We were told by Ian, the welfare officer, that Andy was stable enough to fly home that night so we would need to pack a bag and travel down to Selly Oak hospital at 5am the next morning. There was no question that I would not be there. I wanted to be with him from the second he landed. All that was in my mind was that he would survive. There was no way he could die and leave me without the love of my life. He is the strongest person I have ever met and I knew inside that he would fight.

That car journey to Birmingham was long, and as I had not slept or eaten I was feeling weak but also strangely calm. I knew that we would be there soon and we would find out if Andy had survived the flight. We were taken into the Alex Wing of the hospital and the doctor who had looked after Andy on the flight sat us down and spoke those words that will never leave me: 'He will walk again.'

The time came to visit him in the Critical Care Ward. They had made him comfortable and we were allowed to go and see him. His mother and father went in first, as was only right. Theirs is a different kind of love and as parents, to see their child so close to death and having suffered such a terrible ordeal, was heartbreaking. After they had seen him, I went in. As I was walking down the ward to his bed I felt a rising panic – I simply didn't know what to expect. Then I saw him. He was sedated and there were tubes everywhere. The first thing I noticed was how long and curly his hair was and how tanned his skin was. Despite having a sheet over him, you could see that he had lost his legs and arm. I can honestly say I have never felt such a rush of love in my life. Only then did I give way and start to cry but, they were tears of happiness. He was back and away from that hell-hole! He was going to make it!

The days after that first meeting are a blur. There was a lot of family and friends that came to see him and to see us as well, to support us. When he was in critical care he was sedated and in a coma so I used to sit beside him and talk to him. He would move as if he knew I was there but I couldn't be sure that he really did. Then one day I put my hand on his chest. I could feel his heart racing and he suddenly reached up with his only hand, found mine, and put his on top of it. Then I knew for sure, he did know I was there for him. I also wondered if he would remember what had happened to him when he eventually woke up. I didn't want to have to be the person to tell him about how badly injured he was. Mercifully he had a lovely nurse called Kate who really took care of him and she was wonderful to the family. I think it was she who first spoke to him when they woke him up.

We went in to see him shortly afterwards and at first he thought he was still in Afghanistan and was very distressed. We knew that he was not fully conscious at this point but it still was upsetting all the same. I was so worried that when he came round fully he would not want to be with me anymore and would send me away, but I needn't have worried. As I stood there at the side of his bed and he looked at me, I could see how happy he was at me being there. I knew from that point onwards that NOTHING was ever going to get in our way or stop us!

People say that bad luck comes in threes, so I did not expect two lots of bad news at once. The very same day that I was told about Andy, just after the liaison officer had left, I found a letter waiting for me. At the time I had other things on my mind other than the post but for some reason I opened it. It was from the National Health Service. I had recently attended a local clinic for a routine smear test and these were my results. The letter said that I had to get in touch with the hospital urgently. Obviously, at the time I was not thinking of myself at all so the letter got left on the side. I told my mother about it the next day and she urged me to ring the hospital as soon as I could. At first they wouldn't tell me over the phone but when I explained that I was at Selly Oak Hospital because my partner had stood on a bomb in Afghanistan they changed their mind.

I had pre-cancerous cells Level 3 which means that they are in the advanced stage before they turn cancerous. They had to remove these cells as quickly as possible. There was a chance that some had become cancerous, so they would need to operate as soon as possible to find out. I made the decision not to tell Andy at this point because he needed to be strong and if he knew, he would feel useless because he couldn't do anything. I also wanted to be strong for him and get through it and not worry him if I could possibly avoid it.

Andy's rapid recovery, and in particular the resurgence of his sense of humour and his ability to make me laugh, was a considerable help to me. I don't regard him as inspirational just because he is my husband, but because that is genuinely what he is. He seems to give out positive energy like some sort of human dynamo and all of us picked up on this positive charge.

His visit back to Warminster for the Remembrance Day Service and meeting his old section again was very emotional. Not just for us, his friends and family who had seen how much it cost him being so soon after his injuries, but also for the lads in his section who were really moved at seeing him again. It was around this time that I felt he was at a stage in his recovery where I felt confident enough to tell him about my own problems. I can't tell you how great a joy and relief it was to share my secret. He was, of course, marvellous about it and told me that while it was a huge worry we would fight whatever it was and succeed and that it was just one more obstacle to be overcome. It was a timely moment because I was called in by the doctors to be told that I would require a colposcopy. I was booked in for 29 December.

On Christmas Day we had to go to Whiston Hospital A&E – Andy's drain had come out of the vacuum which was helping to clean the wound in his stump. Unfortunately there was not much they could do; the vacuums were specialised and they hadn't seen anything like it before. We then realised that there was nothing else for it – we would have to drive back to Selly Oak hospital and get them to sort it out. It might be Christmas Day but Andy's health was our priority. On arrival we were told he would have to have another operation and would be discharged on 29 December... the day of my own procedure.

I came home by myself; my mind was torn between

not wanting to leave Andy but I knew I had to have this operation done. I felt vulnerable and I didn't like that feeling; I needed to be as strong for Andy as he was being for me. The day of the operation came and my mum took me in. I knew the following night Andy would be home with me and I was looking forward to a hug. After the operation I came home drowsy from the anaesthetic and in pain. I lay on the couch and minutes later Andy came in with the duty driver. We waited till we were alone and just cried and cried... that was definitely rock bottom, but we had each other and it was only going to get better.

Thankfully, there was not any cancer. The relief was incredible. I would have to be monitored every few months but the worst was over. Many people have said to me 'I wouldn't have coped in your situation'. I would probably be one of those people had I been them looking on. You don't realise how strong love can make you. As they say: 'What does not kill you makes you stronger!'

CHAPTER 13

REHAB, THE PARADE AND THE PARACHUTE

The year 2009 – how was it for you? For me it was not the best. A few high points: my friend Richie's wedding to yet another Claire, for one. But a few lows as well. The small matter of being blown up obviously took a lot of the shine off things, and a week after Claire and Richie's wedding I developed an infection in my stump. Not entirely surprising really – being blown up in Afghanistan not only leaves you with shitty injuries, it also leaves you with a bit of the shitty country as well. The blast drives a load of dust and dirt into your body where it stays forever. It reminds me a bit of that poem, you know the one:

'If I should die, think only this of me;

That there's some corner of a foreign field
That is for ever England.'

Well there is some part of me that is forever Afghanistan.
I will carry it with me to my grave. With all that filth and
crap in there, it's hardly surprising that it caused an
infection. It also set in train a sequence of events that
led, as Claire has already told you, to the lowest point of
our lives, 29 December 2009. Thanks Afghanistan:
forgive me, but if I never hear of you again I will not
shed a tear. Thankfully, as 2010 dawned, almost from
the start things started looking up.

To begin with Claire got the 'all clear'. Although they
had been in the final stages before turning cancerous, the
cells were all removed and, thank God, she just needs to
be monitored now. Then the vacuum device on my
stump did its job and by early January, I went back to
Headley Court to have my new limbs fitted. This gave
me a new purpose, a better focus. I felt that, at last, I was
getting on. One of the really tough parts of the previous
weeks was not so much the problems that I was having,
but seeing how miserable Claire was. Not only did she
have to look after me but she had to face her own fears
and nightmares. I felt particularly bad having to watch
her struggle to get my wheelchair out of the car while I
sat on my arse in the passenger seat. I realised that I had
to get better and be strong for her. I went to Headley Court
in a state of some excitement but I was also nervous. How
would my stumps react to the new limbs? When I first had

them fitted there was still quite a bit of pain in my infected stump. The wound had not completely closed, but I was determined to get up and about.

Not having walked for a while, I found the experience of being back on two legs quite strange. I even got a bit dizzy, but I was adamant that I would persevere. I had last walked back in November between the parallel bars, but then my stump had opened up. Now it was still bleeding but the pain was getting less and less. My left leg had been amputated above the knee and for that I was given a KX06 – a metal leg fitted with a shock absorber. It is a purely mechanical device. The right leg is amputated below the knee and for that I have a carbon fibre socket with a simple straight metal bar down to the foot. Subsequently, I have graduated to the Rolls-Royce of artificial limbs. Called a C-Leg, it is made in Sweden. This employs Bluetooth technology linking it to a computer that means if I stumble it will automatically adjust to help me stand upright again. It's great when I go out on the piss: I never fall over! It's come to something when your leg is smarter than you are!

I stayed at Headley Court having occupational therapy for about six weeks, and whilst there I not only learned how to walk again but also how to write. Remember, my right arm had gone and my left hand had almost lost the middle finger.

My goal was to be able to march on to the parade at Warminster in July when the Duke of Wellington himself would present our Afghan campaign medals. When we were the Duke of Wellington's Regiment he was our Colonel-in-Chief, which was unique, as every other regiment's Colonel-in-Chief is a member of the Royal Family. Now that we were the Yorkshire Regiment, the Duke of York has become our Colonel-in-Chief, but the Duke of Wellington still has a soft spot for his old regiment, now known as 3 Yorks.

It was touch-and-go, but all the staff at Headley Court were magnificent. They were as keen as I was to see me march on. But there were obvious difficulties to overcome. For a start, it would be my first time back in uniform. Did I have any? If I did, would it fit me? Some fairly extensive tailoring would have to take place first. It would also be the first time that I had walked in public. I didn't want to fall over and look an idiot. Clare (yes, I know, yet another one) Painter, my physio at Headley Court, took me out to practise on the tarmac car park.

The day of the parade, 9 July 2010, was a scorcher; the sun blazed down as I marched out with the other members of my section who I hadn't seen since Remembrance Day the previous year. Robbo, my old Section 2IC, followed behind me with a wheelchair, just in case, but I made it out there, in my desert combats and my beret on. The Medal Parade marked the closure of the tour, which was why I was so determined to be there. There were 220 of us on parade, so His Grace presented the medals personally only to the front row of

Burma Company. He came to me last and told me I had done fantastically well to get there. Then he pinned the medal to my chest and patted me on the shoulder. He is quite an old chap and a bit frail and started to lose his balance. He grabbed my arm for support and it was all I could do to remain upright. Fortunately we both made it back OK and finished the parade in fine style. It was a great feeling marching off on my new legs – less than a year after losing both my original ones – in front of Claire, my parents and Karl.

July 2010 also saw the beginning of my charity work. It had started when I was chatting with a girl called Kirsty from the Army Benevolent Fund (ABF). This is a charity specifically concerned with looking after soldiers. I was telling her about a dinner function I had recently attended run by the Dallaglio Foundation. This was founded by the ex-England rugby star, Lawrence Dallaglio. At the dinner, some blokes in uniform were collecting for the charity. I can't remember which unit they were from but it looked like they were having a great night on the free wine! I was sat next to Lawrence himself. I am not into rugby union; I don't see the point of 'line outs' and running into exactly the same place your mate has just been tackled. But I am a massive rugby league fan; the 'Mighty Saints' (St Helens) is my team. However, it was still a great honour to be sat with him, having been a major part of the England team that had won the rugby world cup; and he does a lot of charity work.

I had a question for him that a mate of mine, Martin Blondel, had put me up to ask. Martin had set up a white collar boxing night where volunteer boxers, who were by day bankers and lawyers, could have a laugh punching (or trying to punch) each other for charity. He had managed to get a load of players from all the different rugby league teams to come along and encourage the punters to empty their pockets for the Steve Prescott Foundation. This is another charity set up by the ex-rugby league star Steve Prescott to raise funds for the Christie Hospital in Manchester, which specialises in treating rare forms of cancer, with which Steve, sadly, is himself afflicted. Martin had asked Lawrence Dallaglio to have a bout with the ex-St Helens star Paul Scunthorpe, and for some reason or other it did not happen, so I was to ask Lawrence what went wrong. I duly did and he quickly changed the subject. I think he was scared, but in case Lawrence is reading this, I could be wrong!

Well, when I told Kirsty about the night she mentioned that the ABF were organising a charity parachute on 30 July at the Netheravon parachute school, which is very near Warminster. This was being conducted by The Flying Tigers, the parachute display team from the Princess of Wales' Royal Regiment (PWRR). Apparently it was the first time that the ABF had done a parachute jump to raise money and awareness for the charity. Parachuting was obviously not my bag, so I didn't pay much attention, but then she gave me a rather funny look and asked me straight out whether I would like to take part. I was so surprised I broke the cardinal army rule – never volunteer! Without really thinking I said:

'I'll do it, mate!'

I know; it was a bloody silly trap to fall into, but I had done some static line jumps before, so it was not entirely new to me. I phoned Claire and told her about it. Her response was a bit short.

'You are crazy. Have you not lost enough without jumping out of a plane?'

I don't think she was best pleased.

'So I guess you don't want to do it with me then?' I replied.

Her answer is not printable!

I then explained to her how the guys are the best there is, and that it is more dangerous crossing the road, but she was still not having it. However, we both drove down to Netheravon, and being close to Warminster we got there early. It was a beautiful day with a nice clear blue sky, so I knew the jump would be on. I was on my legs, so I walked over to meet the ABF team and all the guys and one girl from 11 Signals Regiment who were also doing the jump that day. Someone took a few photos then it was time for interviews with the local press and the British Forces Broadcasting Service (BFBS).

I had no idea of the media attention that my participation had attracted. I had assumed that I was just doing a parachute jump like all the rest of the service people there, but every man and his dog seemed to want to talk to me. This was a problem, as I am not good first thing in the morning. I get it from my dad; I need at least ten cups of tea before I can function. There was another problem: I was absolutely bricking it at the realisation that I was actually about to jump out of an aircraft. What the bloody hell was I thinking about when I agreed to do this?

Unfortunately, there were some guys from 3 Yorks there to watch, so there was no going back now. Claire went off to get my wheelchair out of the car and I signed my life away on a disclaimer form. Bit of a bloody cheek really – the army looking to duck out of any injuries I might suffer, considering what had happened to me already! I then met the bloke that I was going to be attached to for the jump. We sat down on some crash mats in the training hall and I took off my legs and put on the jump suit. As you can imagine, I didn't fill the legs, so it was a laugh to see that the good old black masking tape was brought out to tidy away the legs and the right sleeve of the suit. The army is almost entirely held together by black masking tape, so it was fitting that I should be jumping out in an outfit in a similar state.

The instructor went through the drills and what was going to happen. I haven't paid so much attention to a lesson in all my life! Then the time then came to make our way to the plane. I am not going to lie to you: I was shit scared. Even though I had jumped before, my stomach was turning over and I was red hot as I wheeled myself to the plane and the lads lifted me in. If you haven't done a parachute jump, let me explain. There are no seats in the plane and you all sit on the floor facing the rear of the aircraft.

I sat between the legs of my partner. This was getting a lot closer to another man than I would have liked, but we were to get a lot closer before we made it back to the ground! The plane started to taxi down the runway to the take-off position. Everyone was giving it 'big smiles', even me, but I can tell you now that it was a false smile. Inside, my belly was turning over and I thought back to what Claire had said: I must be crazy. Fortunately, I had 100% confidence in my instructor. He had done over 1,000 jumps, so knew what he was doing – at least I thought, and hoped, so!

The plane started to speed down the runway and my oppo pulled me onto his knee, clipped us together and pulled down on the straps. I reached up to check their tension for myself and thought that they seemed a bit loose. I nodded at them to my instructor but he motioned at me not to worry; everything was fine! I watched the altimeter on his wrist going up until it reached 11,000 feet. I thought that we would be off now, and looked out of the door which was covered by a see-through plastic roller shutter. All I could see was clouds. Then I looked at the altimeter again; it was now on 12,000 feet. What the fuck! When are we going to jump? I stared at it intently; it kept rising until it reached 14,000 feet and only then did they finally fling open the door. We started shuffling towards it and I looked out again but could only see white clouds, not the ground. I know this sounds weird, but it was a good job that I only had one arm and no legs, because otherwise I am pretty sure that I would have got up and run to the other side of the fuselage and clung on to something secure. Instead I was completely helpless. The instructor snatched my head back and we were out.

We rolled slowly around in the air in perfect silence, other than the rushing of the air past my ears, and plummeted earthwards. My sense of fear immediately changed to one of exhilaration. I have only ever had the same buzz when I did 175mph on my GSX-R 750 motorbike (on a private road, of course). It was awesome; a massive adrenaline rush that I had thought I would never experience again. I was falling at 120mph for 45 amazing seconds, watching the ground coming up towards me. Another team member with a camera strapped to his helmet filmed us on the way down. I was trying to smile and give the thumbs up but falling that fast, the wind force makes you pull all kinds of crazy faces. Then all too quickly it was over and we were yanked back up into the air: the instructor had pulled the ripcord and opened the parachute. It was now just a case of floating back down to earth and landing the both of us. This was accomplished very smoothly and we settled on the ground like a roosting swan.

As soon as we hit the ground the parachute was gathered up and the press rushed over with a barrage of questions. I was still buzzing from the jump, so talked total rubbish, but it was a really great day and I think we raised about £12,000. I had now got a real taste for charity work.

I have a very soft spot for the ABF. They have been of great help to me and Claire. It was they who paid for and fitted a ramp, and widened the doorway to our old house, and they have been similarly helpful to us in our new place. (Unlike some service charities they don't make a song and dance about what they do, they just get on and help people, and if this book encourages you to make a donation to a service charity, can I please ask that it is to the ABF). They were delighted with my rather simple contribution and I started to do more and more for them to help publicise their fund-raising campaign. This gave me a taste for the work and it seemed to be something I was quite good at. I suppose it is hard to refuse a bloke with no legs and only one arm asking you for money. It also taught me that it pays to go with your first instinct. If it sounds like a good idea, go for it. You are a long time dead!

This explains why, when an ex-soldier friend of mine from St Helens later asked me how I would fancy joining him and some others on their charity motorbike ride from Land's End to John O'Groats, I thought that although that might be a bit tricky, as I only had one arm, why not? So it was set. We would set out on a five-day charity fundraiser bike tour over the course of the August Bank Holiday weekend of 2010, from one end of the country to the other. No big challenge you might think, but consider this: at that time I had only just got steady on my new feet, I was yet to master my prosthetic arm, and I had not ridden a bike since before deploying to Afghanistan. Before I left, I owned a Suzuki 750; it was a thing of rare beauty and I missed it like hell. I used to love simply starting it up, revving it like mad and then taking it for a real ball-breaking spin on a convenient motorway. Obviously that was a thing of the past and Claire was pretty determined it would remain there. She was also about as enthusiastic about this motorbike ride idea as she was about my parachute jump. I suppose she had a point. How was I going to be able to ride a bloody motorbike? I could barely stay on a chair let alone the pillion of a high performance road machine.

However, I was able to reassure her. A company called Boom Trikes, in Worsley, had kindly volunteered to loan us a two-seater 500cc trike that they would adapt to take my collapsible wheelchair, as well as shifting all the throttle controls to the left-hand side along with a foot-operated servo brake. This was brilliant – it meant I could ride the bike confidently and with ease. I couldn't bank it into a bend at 90mph like I could on my old Gizzer, but I would give it a bloody good go. The trike had a huge bench seat that I could fit on easily. There was just one problem: with me sitting in one place on a road journey, the cheeks of my arse went numb. This gave us the name of our event: the 'Numbumrun'!

I knew that I would need help with the wheelchair, so

I asked my cousin Karl if he wanted to come along for the trip. As I expected, he jumped at the chance. He is a big fucker and I was a little concerned that we would be doing wheelies, but it worked out fine. We were like Maverick and Goose – he was my wing man, or more like my bitch, depends how you look at it. We took the bike out for a couple of test rides, swapping over so that we could both get used to the feel of the machine. We also needed to work out how we could communicate with each other during the ride. We eventually arrived at a sort of understanding. Essentially this was that I would fall asleep while I was pillion, but when I was driving, Karl would be screaming at me with terror on every overtake and approach to a bend. I thought that this arrangement was fine, but Karl wasn't so happy with it.

We spent most of the time up to our departure raising money with organiser Cliff Williams and his partner Colette, along with the other members of the team – Simon, Big John Mac, and PC Gareth Ollie. We would go to various biker events to help raise awareness and to sell raffle tickets. I say 'we' but this was mainly the team minus me. I had got another infection in my right stump. That Afghan shit deep inside the wound was still trying to hurt me and it needed to be scraped out and cleaned so that I could crack on with my rehab.

The charity ride plan was to sell raffle tickets for donated prizes, along with collection buckets. I have to say that the generosity of the British public toward injured soldiers is incredible and, in my view, not spoken of highly enough. In particular, the biker fraternity were brilliant; so generous to us, with many of them signing up to take part in some part of the run. Indeed, some even came along for the whole ride... yes all of it!

We set off on the Friday morning, leaving Warrington at 5am. The kit was loaded and the tarp was secured over the bike on the trailer. Cliff had had some banners made up for the van and it all looked cracking. The drive down flew by as we chatted and got to know each other. John Mac was a 60-year-old ex-squaddie, so we got on like a house on fire. He is a cross between Kojak and Big Daddy; a great laugh and full of stories. Simon worked at BMW so I was tapping him up for car advice, and the other John was our photographer for the trip. We soon reached Bristol and had a good fill-up at ASDA; their breakfasts hit the spot. We then motored on down to Penzance, where we were staying for the first night. A lovely couple donated their hotel for the lot of us free of charge. They were incredible and had us up early the next day for breakfast and the start of the challenge. They made sure that we were well fed and on departure they donated the entire cost of our stay to the cause. This was very touching, so if you are ever in Penzance check out The Guest House – you will not be disappointed.

During the short drive over to Land's End the discussion was about how many people would be there to see us off. The suggestions ranged from zero to about ten, so you can imagine how stunned we were to see that about 40 bikers had turned up to ride out with us. Checks were made and Cliff made a brief speech to the crowd, revving to go. We took the last of the photographs and started our journey. The game plan was to have Gareth up front on his police bike, with John Mac and Simon leading the ride, and me and Karl on the trike just behind. John and Simon were riding 125cc Vespas. They were smartly branded, adding style to the convoy, although over the five days we would get sick of seeing John's arse and Simon kicking his legs out looking like he was about to fall off.

The route on day one was to cover Land's End to Battlesbury Barracks in Warminster. This was my home and it is also the home of 3 Yorks – The Dukes – so I knew the way like the back of my hand. The plan was that I would start and end each day's ride, with Karl swapping over every 50 miles. As it happened, each day was broken up roughly into four or five stops, so it was a good plan. Whoever was pillion was in touch with Cliff in the control vehicle. He was in touch with Gareth who was in touch with the local police authority. The plan of putting Gareth up front was a genius: it enabled us to have a police escort virtually the whole route. This allowed us to run red lights while the police went on ahead to clear junctions along the route.

When we arrived on the outskirts of Warminster we changed over so that I could ride into Warminster to meet the local Mayor and the Town Crier. At the RV point where the change was to be made we were met by Captain Nick Wilson and a few of the lads from Camp. It was great to see them, and our convoy grew as we got into Warminster. Unknown to us, word had got out regarding our arrival time and the people of Warminster had set up a welcome party. The town was packed, with people lining the streets, clapping and cheering as we arrived. We pulled into a car park where there was a local television news crew who wanted us to do interviews for the regional news programmes.

I was very moved to spot my own commanding officer, Lieutenant Colonel Tom Vallings. He was stood in full uniform clapping us in. When we parked up he came over and gripped my hand and said, 'Bloody great effort Reidy, well done!' Karl jumped off and offered his seat to the colonel who looked a bit shocked but jumped on. He waved an arm like Monty and shouted:

'Off to Camp!'

With that we set off for the barracks, me driving the trike with the colonel on the back. The look on the face of the sentry as he raised the barrier to let us in was brilliant. He didn't know whether to salute or just wave us through.

We ended up in the NAAFI where the Dukes had laid on a massive barbecue. Colonel Tom served us all with our scoff and we enjoyed the craic and just a very few cold beers. It had been a great day. Big John went back for seconds; he made us laugh when he saw the colonel serving up the food and just said 'Thanks Chef', before giggling and sneaking off stuffing his face.

Day two was a long day. We set off early and I was knackered. I nearly fell asleep at one point and Karl was tapping me on my head to keep me awake. As before, at our first scheduled stop there were about 50 bikers who wanted to join us for the run. It was a long run but we didn't mind – we were heading home. That night's stop was at Preston Barracks and prior to that we would stop at Millennium Motorcycles in St Helens. They had donated the scooters that Simon and John were riding.

We knew we must be getting close to St Helens because the heavens opened. However, we didn't mind as we headed up to Warrington where the BMW dealership which had donated the minibus was based, along with Simon and Cliff. As we approached the M62, Gareth pulled us together, controlling the speed of the convoy. Unknown to us there was a roadblock in place ahead. I say roadblock, in fact there were four police BMW X5s across all four lanes of the motorway. As we dropped onto it, Gareth waved us through and it was all ours – we had the M62, on a Saturday afternoon at 3pm, all to ourselves. It was simply incredible and very, very moving. We spotted a police officer on the bridge overhead with a camera. He must have got a great photo. It really was brilliant. The last time a copper had taken a photo of me on the M62 I got three points on my licence!

The arrival at Millennium was very emotional. All of our family members were there to greet us, along with a few bands and another barbecue. We had a great couple of hours posing for shots before heading off to Preston and our beds for the night. Once we got settled in we made a point of going to the local pub for a few beers. It was a good time to meet and chat to the convoy riders. And it was only then that we realised there were three people who had made the whole journey with us that far. These heroes were Big Colin, Dave and Carl. They have kept in touch with us to this day.

Day three was epic! The route was Preston to Dumbarton, which took us over Shap Fell in the Lake District. The countryside and views were stunning but the long rides were starting to take their toll. It was good to swap over with Karl but the cold was getting into my legs and I was feeling very tired. We were due to stay at another barracks and the facilities were adequate, but that was all. They were certainly not the comforts of the hotel back in Penzance. Once we arrived, Karl went on a recce to see what the rooms were like. By this time we knew that Big John snored, and I mean snored! It was like someone was slaughtering a pack of dogs... he denied this, but Karl knew we needed somewhere quiet.

Mandy and Phil, a couple doing the run in honour of their friend Bootey who was killed in Afghanistan in the same year, had started to keep an eye out for us. Mandy wanted somewhere to doss down away from all the men who were on the ride. She pulled Karl over and said that she had something for him. He was a bit confused at first until she explained that she had found the sergeants' mess. It was a plush, decorated room with chesterfield sofas and a cabinet full of whisky. Karl immediately bagged it for us both. It beat sleeping in the sports hall, and it was far away enough from John's nightly nasal recital.

We knew that we were getting close to the end, which was just as well because while spirits were still really high, people were getting very tired. Cliff and Colette were doing an amazing job keeping us to the schedule. He would regularly radio either Karl or me to check that we were OK. We left Dumbarton en route to Inverness. Cliff told us that if we thought the Lakes were impressive, this next leg would blow us away; he was not wrong. Karl had never been that far north but I had climbed Ben Nevis so I knew how great the scenery was. Besides the views, it was incredible at how many people made the effort to be a part of my ride. Cliff had done a great job and because of his tireless campaigning and fundraising, word of our 'Numbumrun' had got out to a huge number of people, and we were very well supported on our journey.

We arrived at Glen Coe, and if you have never been, then you must make a point of going because it is truly stunning: massive open plains with huge monumental rocks overhanging the roads. Having had enough of looking at John's arse on the leading Vespa, I decided to try and overtake the scooters. I gave the throttle a wrench and we nearly took off. Karl screamed like a girl but I loved the rush of the ride and being free on a bike again. It is a bit of a cliché, but unless you have sampled it you will never know how good it feels.

There is a viewing point along the road where we pulled in to admire the view. A coach party of American tourists were taking pictures when we arrived, and they were stunned when they learned what I had been through and that I was riding the trike. They insisted on taking more pictures of us all as well as the view. Then one of my volunteer riders came over to introduce himself. I had noticed him from the first. He looked as cool as fuck dressed in jeans, cowboy boots and a Stars and Stripes helmet with goggles, and was riding a soft-tail Harley Davidson – a really beautiful machine. He looked as if he had just stepped out of a re-make of *Easy Rider*. His name was Tim Bigelow (no, I am not making this up), an American ex-serviceman now living in the UK. He had joined us on day one but his first bike, an old BMW, broke down, so he went back home and got out his Harley. The guy is a legend.

We progressed onwards toward our next stopover point at Fort George in Inverness. An epic journey: glorious surroundings and the sun blazing down, what more could you ask? Before we got to Inverness we stopped at the Commando Memorial at Spean Bridge and laid a wreath. All-in-all it had been a great experience and we raised a lot of money for the charity.

On arrival at John O'Groats there was a mini-bus to take us home and a low-loader for the trike.

Besides charity work, my enforced idleness while I waited for appointments at Headley Court meant that I could follow up a number of things that I had not had the time to do when I was serving. One of these was music. I had first met the group Sound of Guns a few months before I went to Afghanistan. Nathan, the guitarist, worked with Karl in Liverpool and they were booked to do a gig in the city. Karl asked if Claire and I fancied coming along. I wasn't a big music fan then, I only owned about seven CDs and they were by groups like The Doors, The Who and Pink Floyd, and I loved to drive to the *Top Gun* soundtrack. 'Danger Zone' is a great number if you are in a rush to get somewhere.

However, I thought it was a good excuse to get out on the piss and as I had never been to a gig like this before I thought 'Why not?' The concert was on the top floor of an old building in Seal Street. There were four of us: me, Claire, Karl and Karl's wife. First impressions were not good. The bar only sold cans of Red Stripe or that disgusting Blue WKD alcopop. As I wasn't 16, I went for the Red Stripe!

The guys from the band came over to greet us. They were all dressed in skin-tight jeans, had long hair and were about seven feet tall, apart from Andy the lead singer. They said their hellos and then went backstage. When they came on there was a real buzz about the place. By this time I had taken a few Red Stripes on board and was really getting into it. 'Rack and Ruin' was their best number, and after the gig I bought their CD and played it almost constantly from then on. I had it on in the car and in the house, and the words from some of the tracks started to really stick in my head; I could relate to them. When I went to Afghanistan I took my iPod with the CD on it and when I got downtime I would put it on and close my eyes and think back to that night out with Claire and remember what a great night it was.

When I got injured, Karl told the group and they sent me a signed LP and some T-shirts, which was ace. I put one on when Prince Charles came to see me, so I could get a picture of me wearing it with him, but somehow the picture got lost. The Prince arrived about a month after I was injured, when I was in Selly Oak. He just turned up one day with his driver, pulled up a chair and chatted to me and the others for a while. I told him all about the bike ride I was planning, and then when I met him again at the Millies in 2010, he asked me how it had gone. It was really nice that he'd remembered.

Anyway, I listened to Sound of Guns all though my rehab, and the words on each track really helped me push myself forward. When Karl told me the group was playing at the same venue again I was really keen to go and see them. I really needed the buzz of hearing them live – but I was in my wheelchair. How would I get up all the stairs? I doubted they had a lift, but Karl said that he would get me in there somehow. On the night of the gig we arrived at the entrance of the club. The doors were guarded by some pretty big bouncers, which was actually a good job: Karl got me over his shoulder and the doormen picked up my chair and carried it up the three flights of steep stairs to the concert hall.

It was an amazing gig. It was all just as I remembered it from the first time, apart from me missing a few limbs of course! The lads gave me a shout out and all came over to say hello after the gig. Then we all went to The Swan pub around the corner, a small place full of 'wannabe' rock stars and groupies. They serve a drink in there called 'Wobbly Bobs'. It is a strong pint, about 7% proof which Nathan described as a crazy man's drink... as he was knocking back his third. I told him that was weeny league. If he wanted a real crazy man's drink he should try something I came across in Canada called 'The Paralyser'. It consists of half-and-half milk and coke into which you pour four shots of vodka. Drink that and I guarantee that it will do exactly what it says on the tin, namely paralyse you! Yes, you guessed it, me and Nathan had a few after we managed to talk the barman into giving us some of his milk he was keeping for his evening brews. I later heard that Nathan's mum was not very impressed with The Paralyser. Apparently when he got home he threw up all over her and then used her new white towels to clean up. Rock stars! Bet Ozzy Osborne never did that!

CHAPTER 14

THE MILLIES

After all the excitement of the Medals Parade and the Numbum trip, I was in dire need of a holiday, so Claire, myself and couple of other mates hired a canal barge for a week's boating. This was really great; so peaceful just chugging gently along, looking at the beautiful countryside gliding past. The holiday would take in Claire's birthday and I had decided some time before that it would be the ideal occasion for me to pop the question about marriage. I was determined to do this properly, so when I was at Headley Court, I sought out Clare Painter who had done such a great job getting me fit for the Medals Parade. When I asked my Claire to marry me I was determined to do it down on one knee. The thing was, I only *had* one knee, and getting down on it was tricky, but not as tricky as getting back up. To do that I needed another knee or a leg that would flex and let me push my body up off the ground.

There was nothing else for it – I was going to have to get down on my artificial knee. Prosthetic legs are not really designed with aspiring suitors in mind, so that posed a real problem. Fortunately, Claire P was master of it and on 7 August 2010, at the Cross Keys Pub in Runcorn, I managed to pop the question kneeling on one knee like a real Romeo.

There was quite a funny prelude to this event. Someone in the group had suggested that as it was Claire's birthday we should have a party and, not knowing what I had planned, suggested a pirate theme. She was a bit disappointed when I rather curtly rejected the idea. I had enough worries about making a tit of myself when I proposed as it was, without adding being dressed as a bloody pirate! Well I did it and she accepted my proposal. It did occur to me that after all that effort if she had said no I would probably have taken one of my bloody legs off and smacked her with it, but she said yes. As a birthday present, and in a fit of dizzy joy at her accepting my proposal, I asked her to name her dearest wish and I would grant it. I was a bit taken aback when she said she wanted to go on a world cruise but there it was, me and my big mouth. There was no backing out of it so I had no other option than to say yes. However, it did give me the chance of cracking a very bad joke. When she made her request I looked at her and said:

'OK, we will go on a world cruise – but it will cost me an arm and a leg!'

How we laughed.

In fact a cruise was a bloody good idea. Flying did not appeal. In any case, I was riddled with shrapnel and bits of Afghanistan and would have set off all the security alarms. I spoke to the powers that be and the unit was more than happy to give me 12 weeks' leave. Then it was all down to my doctor, Colonel Phillips. He gave us the thumbs up, so on 23 September 2010, two days after my 34th birthday, we set off for Southampton with a suitcase bulging with medications – and a couple of spare legs – and went aboard the *Oriana*. She sailed that night and Madeira was the first destination. We had an absolute ball, although we hadn't realised that we would be the youngest passengers by at least 30 years. I think they told me the average age on board was 67, and sadly a number popped their clogs en route!

With me rolling around on my artificial legs I look pretty nautical on dry land as it is, so I found the motion of the ship at sea pretty normal. Claire, poor kid, suffered a bit from sea sickness. We started to attract a lot of attention, although I wasn't the only disabled bloke on board. There was a chap called Mark who was paralysed from the waist down after a farming accident. It just goes to show, you might think you are hard done by, but there is always somebody worse off than you. At least I could walk.

Our route took us from Madeira across the Atlantic to the Panama Canal, then Curacao, Acapulco, San Francisco, Hong Kong, Thailand and Singapore. We got off at most stops but I was disappointed at the lack of disabled facilities. We in Britain are pretty good, but other countries seem to make no effort at all.

I started to swim again. As you can imagine, swimming without any legs and only one arm could be a rather dangerous pastime, but Headley Court had sorted me out and I was very happy in the water. Highlights of the trip were snorkelling over the Great Barrier Reef and an elephant ride in Thailand. On the first anniversary of my injury, 13 October, we were in San Francisco, so that date is now linked to a much happier event.

One day, the Cruise Director came to our table and told us that a number of the passengers had asked him about us and were very interested in hearing our story. He invited us to take part in a sort of interview meeting one evening. We both agreed, expecting that perhaps three or four might turn up. It was advertised in the ship's daily newsletter, and when we arrived we were gobsmacked to find an audience of well over 800. We outdid Sarajevo hero General Michael Rose who was also on board to give a series of lectures, and Edwina Currie who was also there on a paid jolly. This experience and the great response that I got from it gave me the idea that this could be the basis of a new career after leaving the army, and so it has proved. It really gave me the confidence to do more public speaking, which has helped no end with the talks I now do in schools and at corporate events.

One place we visited that I found particularly moving was Pearl Harbor in Hawaii, the site of the devastating attack by the Japanese on the US naval base on 7 December 1941. More than 1,000 US military personnel were lost when the *USS Arizona* was bombed and sunk in just one of the raids, and the remains of many of its crew are still incarcerated on board. As such, it is a National War Grave, and the whole site is very disturbing place to visit.

Happier memories are of dinner at the Captain's table and then being taken up onto the bridge and being allowed to blow the horn as we sailed out of port. We did meet one other couple of similar age, Pauline and Colin. They were getting married aboard and in a gesture that quite literally rocked me on my legs Colin asked me to be his best man. I was very honoured and fortunately, being at sea where the booze was complimentary, organising his stag night was not too difficult! We were really enjoying ourselves but something was about to happen that would really blow our socks off.

The Cruise Director came to see me again while I was in the gym on the treadmill. He told me that the *Sun* newspaper had been on the phone asking me to call them back immediately. He was able to organise this for me and I spoke to someone who gave me the astounding news that I had been put up by the ABF for one of the newspaper's Millie Awards. These awards, started by the Prince of Wales and sponsored by the *Sun*, are awarded annually to military units and personnel who have been nominated under a number of different categories. I was up for the award for 'overcoming adversity'. This was all fine and dandy but I had a more pressing issue to overcome. I was on board the *Oriana* in the Mediterranean and the awards ceremony was in the Imperial War Museum in London. How was I going to get there? Fortunately, someone had thought of that.

Claire and I disembarked in Athens and flew back to Heathrow. As I had predicted, getting through airport security was not easy. My alcohol sprays that I need to disinfect my prosthetics caused a lot of grief. Nevertheless, we made it back and there was a taxi waiting to take us to our Quarter in Warminster. There, somebody had organised a tailor to kit me out in a proper Number 2 Dress uniform. This was fortunate, as cruising is all very well but it is not a good place to lose weight. I was now decidedly portly and my old uniform was too small.

Once that had been done, some people from the *Sun* turned up to make a film of me driving a car, swimming and generally having a good time. This was a cause of some embarrassment later, as I shall explain. You will note that I mentioned driving a car. I had started taking lessons back in February and the DVLA had organised an assessment of my skills and decided that I could keep my licence. I had some money from the sale of a property and I used it to buy myself a Jag. Sounds a bit flash, but remember I had had to kiss goodbye to my motorbike, so I got a fast car instead. A local company called BAS Hand Controls converted it for me and it was great because it opened up so many more opportunities for me and Claire.

Anyway, back to the Millies. We were very honoured to be told that the Prime Minister, David Cameron, had invited all the nominees to Number 10 Downing Street for lunch. We asked how we were to get there and they told us that a taxi would pick us up from our Quarter at 08.00 in the morning. We sat there in our gladrags expectantly but no taxi arrived. By 09.00, I was starting to get worried. I rang the liaison guy at the *Sun* who went ballistic. He told us to call up another taxi at once from our nearest local firm – the *Sun* would pay the bill – and it fairly raced up the M3 to London. We arrived only 30 minutes late.

At Number 10, we met the other two nominees in my category. One was a Royal Marine and the other an airman. Claire, being the very polite but rather naïve girl that she is, asked them how they had found all the filming. There was an awkward silence then one of them asked, 'what filming'? Neither of them had been contacted, none of their details had been taken. It was a rather tricky moment because we all suddenly realised that I must have won. I felt there was little point trying to hide this, so I came out and said:

'Well guys, I think I have won this.'
And so it proved.

The awards themselves were an incredible experience. The ceremony was held in the presence of their Royal Highnesses the Prince of Wales and the Duchess of Cornwall. Beforehand we were all put up in the Crowne Plaza Hotel in St James's and we were taken to the venue by luxury coach. When we arrived it was like something out of the Oscars. A long red carpet stretched from where we were parked into the building and it was flanked by cheering crowds. We progressed down the carpet like film stars; paparazzi photographers scampered about us taking pictures. The bulbs flashed, the shutters clicked and the crowds cheered. It was bloody marvellous.

When we got to the door we were met by someone from the *Sun*. He knew the manner of men he was dealing with, as the first thing he did was to eye us all sternly and warn us to go easy on the free champagne. I took him at his word, which was just as well, as the winners had to walk up on to the stage to receive their prize and give a speech. I was scared shitless. Would I make it? What was I going to say? All too quickly my category came up. The persons presenting this particular award were Jeremy Clarkson and Myleene Klass. When they came on I now knew it was definitely my award because Clarkson was someone I had long wanted to meet and I had told the *Sun* people this. The envelope was opened and my name called. I think I made a pretty good fist of acting surprised. Then came the rather cringe-making video. I really couldn't bring myself to watch it. At the end, I got up from my table and set off on the long walk to the stage. Everybody was on their feet clapping and cheering. I climbed up to join Clarkson. There was no handrail, steps or ramp but I made it. Jeremy handed me the award and I got a kiss from Myleene, which was quite a good experience. She looked and smelled gorgeous.

I then went over to the podium and looked out at the crowd that had by now fallen silent, waiting for me to speak. It was a very strange moment. So much had happened to me over the last 18 months. Now here I was about to address an audience that contained their Royal Highnesses, the Prime Minister and a shedful of other celebs like Andrew Lloyd Webber, Cesc Fabregas, David Beckham and David Jason. Also, there was Ian Lister, my welfare officer, and some of the crew from Headley Court. I looked down at them all, at Claire and the other nominees. Here I was, a fighting corporal from 3 Yorks, about to get an award in front of all these nobs. That was great, we all like to get awards, but this was one that I really wished that I did not qualify for; but I did and I had bloody well won it. I had faced my enemy and for now I had triumphed over it. The Taliban had tried to cut me down but I had managed to pick myself up and with the help of friends and family I was still living, still fighting and above all – still standing tall.

CHAPTER 15

STANDING TALL

A lot has happened since I won the Millie Award in 2010 and I feel like my life has gone from strength to strength.

Claire and I were married on 10 September 2011. This was my main goal apart from being able to walk again. Claire is very organized and wanted every detail of the wedding sorted out, which is good because I am the opposite – very disorganized – so I left it to her. But when we went looking for a venue as soon as we stepped inside the Wrightington Hotel in Chorley, not far from where we live, we both knew it was the place we wanted to get married in. It is a fantastic place and all our guests could stay over. In fact, the whole day was amazing, especially being able to walk down the aisle with Claire, who looked sensational in her wedding dress. All our friends and family were there as well as some great mates from the regiment including Tom and Lulu and Sam and Ellie. Tom was CO when I was injured and we are good friends now. It's funny, because I have been stood to attention in front of a few commanding officers over the years for different misdemeanors, but until the wedding had never stood at the bar with one! Tom's mum, Tessa, also became a good friend when I was at Headley Court. She lived close by and used to make me wonderful cakes, and I would go round for tea when I was on rehab. Sam, as you know, was my OC and again, like Tom, he has become a great friend.

I had asked Karl to be my best man. I know he is my cousin but he is also my best mate so it wasn't a difficult decision. When it came to planning the stag do I think Karl was a bit worried it was going to be a crazy weekend somewhere abroad but I decided to keep it local so more of my mates could afford to come. We went to the races and although to be honest I am not much of a gambler, it was a great day. I thought a good way of saving money for everyone was for them all to crash at mine for the weekend. I didn't realize at the time how many lads would be staying. At one point there was someone asleep in the hot tub (this is very dangerous, I should add, folks!) and one guy asleep on the stairs, which can't have been comfortable.

Claire decided she was going to Barcelona with about twenty friends on the same weekend – she wasn't daft, was she! This meant that I had to make sure the house was tidy for when she got back, but luckily I got someone I know to come in and clean and she was none the wiser.

At the end of March 2012 Claire went on a hen weekend to Brighton with a group of her friends and on the Saturday morning I had a phone call from her. Nothing could have braced me for what she had to tell me... She was pregnant.

She had suspected it for a while but having gone away with her friends she decided she couldn't wait any longer, because if she had drunk alcohol while pregnant she might have harmed the baby. When she told me this news I was so incredibly happy. I thought back to the day I was injured. I had been so unsure of the future, and here I was now with my wife expecting our baby.

We decided to find out the sex of the baby so we could be more organized and plan everything. At sixteen weeks we booked a private scan and confirmed what we had thought and hoped for... a baby boy. Don't get me wrong: we would have been so happy to have a girl, but having a baby boy meant that he would carry my first name, William, like my father and both my grandfathers.

While Claire was pregnant we had a call from the producer for the Hairy Bikers. They were making a programme called *Everyday Gourmets* and wanted to do a show with us, in which we would make a surprise meal to thank friends who have helped us over the years since I was injured. Of course we jumped at this chance. Filming took place in August 2012 and it was such a great few days. The Bikers are genuinely lovely blokes and we had such a laugh with them. They have written the foreword for this book, as you will have seen, and I am very proud to call them my mates. The meal was a barbecue, which we thought was a great idea, as we love a good BBQ with mates – the only hard part was picking which of all our amazing friends to invite. The food we made was outstanding, and not your typical BBQ fare: we had pork belly and hogget with different beers to match each course. Claire was disappointed because, being pregnant, she couldn't have any of the beer on offer!

William was born at 8.48 pm on 30 November 2012 by caesarian section, and I was at Claire's side the whole time. He weighed in at a whopping 9lb 1½ ounces, but he was perfect in every way. It was the best feeling I have ever had, holding William and looking at Claire. She was exhausted, but I could see she was as happy as I was. I then had to go home as it was late and I could not stay on the ward. I thought about going to my local for a pint with Karl and my dad, but I was very tired by then. In the end I had a few cans and slept on the couch to save time coming downstairs in the morning so that I could get to the hospital quicker. They came home from the hospital after two days, but Claire had to go back in for two days as she had a nasty infection and needed IV antibiotics. This meant she was away from the baby, which she found extremely distressing. Claire's mum came and stayed at the house with me to help me look after him, which was a great help as I could not have managed on my own in the first few days. I did take William in to the hospital to see Claire as often as I could, for I knew she couldn't bear to be away from him; however, she needed to get better first.

My motivational speaking career has really taken off. I talk to all kinds of people on all sorts of occasions, from after-dinner speaking to addressing schools, businesses and hospitals. But as you know I really enjoy rugby league, so when I am asked to speak to clubs it's always a great honour. I have given talks for Saints, Huddersfield Giants and Doncaster Knights, but my best talk to date was for Warrington Wolves before one of their games against Wigan Warriors. I felt nervous because it was a big game for the team and because it was being filmed for a documentary for More4 called *Our Soldiers: Return to Civvy Street* in which I was taking part. The talk went really well. The guys all seemed to enjoy it – and more importantly, they beat Wigan!

Speaking to people who need a bit of advice on how to move forward with their lives really makes me feel good about myself. After being injured I didn't think that I would find a job again that I enjoyed, but I take so much out of speaking to people and making a difference. I have recently started a company called AIM (Amputation Inspiration Motivation) with my friend Steve Cruse, and I hope that in the coming years it will give me a long-term job and a secure future for Claire and William. True, the money I received from the MOD and my own insurance policy has bought me a nice bungalow with a big garden for William to play in, but I still need to pay my bills.

However, despite my family and my speaking career, I decided that I didn't have enough on, so over drinks with some friends we decided that we would open a bar in St Helens. At first we made a bit of a joke of it, but when it actually came down to it we thought, 'Let's do this'. We found a building in Duke Street that used to be a cinema years ago – in fact, back in the sixties The Beatles actually played a couple of gigs, there so it was an ideal location, with St Helens being my home town. For obvious reasons we named it 'Cinema Bar', and it opened in August 2013. It's going really well at the moment, and I particularly like local people coming in and talking to me.

I was asked to take part in a charity single for the ABF The Soldiers Charity by a St Helens-based group called Titors Insignia. The song is called 'Freedom Fighter' and I was really happy to be asked. Once the video had been completed the single was launched and made the charts, and I hope it will do really well. We held the launch at Cinema Bar and it was a cracking night.

What's next? Well, in the autumn I completed the Washington DC marathon on my bike in 4 hours and 20 minutes, which was a fantastic time of which I'll admit

I'm really proud. While there I got to visit the Pentagon and met the WWF wrestler Million Dollar Man. It was such a great trip and I'm hoping to take some time off for it again next year.

I'm taking part in a challenge for a remarkable charity called the Pilgrim Bandits. Founded by a group of Special Forces veterans, it has, in their words, 'the sole aim of using our unique training and experience to help and inspire wounded soldiers to live life to the full'. They raise money to send the lads on great holidays and trips away, and they are for ever asking me to do sky dives for them, but this trip in 2014 is going to be one of my biggest challenges yet... Before that, though, we are flying out to Dubai to do a sky dive and have a good few days out there. It's not every day you get an opportunity like that, is it?

I know one day I will have to slow down and take things a bit easier, but while I've been given a second chance at life I'm not going to waste a moment of it.

POSTSCRIPT
FOR WILLIAM

William is over a year old now, a happy, healthy boy with a lot of character. When he is quite a lot older I will be able to discuss with him what happened to me, and answer all his questions as best I can, but I wanted to give him something while he is still very young that might help him understand what happened to me, and why, and what I think about it all. So I wrote a short piece about it all, that can be read to him or which, one day, he will be able to read for himself (and then he will ask me lots of questions, because small children are really, really good at that...). It is oversimplified, of course, but I hope that it will help him, and perhaps others who may, unfortunately, find themselves in a similar position. Here it is:

What happened to Daddy

When Daddy was a little boy just like you, he used to play outside a lot running around with his friends, and his favourite game was playing soldiers. He had a toy gun and used to dress up in his grandad's old army clothes and make dens and pretend he was in the army. When he left school all he wanted to do was be a soldier, so he went to the army office in town and met a real soldier, a sergeant, who told him all about the army and what they do. Daddy was very excited and asked the sergeant if he could join, and the sergeant said there were some tests that he had to pass so they would know he was fit enough to join. So he sat at a computer and started the test. If Daddy had worked harder at school he would not have worried about the test but he used to mess about in class. Now he realised how important school is. When he had finished the test they weighed him on some scales and measured his height. Luckily he passed all the tests and was allowed to join the army.

After all his training he was sent to Northern Ireland to join the rest of his regiment. He loved it there, going out in helicopters and out on patrol, making sure everyone was safe. He was also sent to Kosovo and to Iraq twice to keep people safe from the bad men that are in those countries.

Daddy had been in the army for 13 years and loved his job so much he was going to stay in for 22 years, but in 2009 the army asked him to go to join other British soldiers in a dangerous country called Afghanistan, where there are groups of bad man who won't let children go to school or women go shopping, and who make the men grow fields of plants to make drugs so the bad men make lots of money. It was Daddy's job to go out on patrols with his friends in the army and look for the bad men so they could be arrested and taken to the police station. The bad men did not like the army being there and used to shoot at the soldiers and hide bombs under the ground to hurt them. It was very important for the soldiers and army to be there because then children could go to school and mums and dads could enjoy working, growing food and shopping for things, just like we do.

Daddy had been there for three months, enjoying his work keeping the people safe, but on a very sunny day he went on a patrol with his army friends to see if any bad men were about, and stepped on a bomb hidden under the ground. There was a huge BANG! and lots of dust and dirt went up in the air. Daddy lay on his back with dust all around him, and because the bang was so loud he could not hear anything. He looked down and could not see his legs, and one of his arms was twisted behind his back so he could not see that either. He was not in any pain, for it did not hurt. Some of his friends, the other soldiers, started to put bandages on his legs

203

and arm and sent a radio message for a helicopter to come and take him to hospital so the doctors and nurses could make him better.

Next day he was back in England in hospital and Mummy came to see him. The doctor told her that the bomb had taken off both Daddy's legs and his right arm. Mummy was very upset, but loved Daddy so much that she was going to help him get better and then they would get married. Daddy was not angry at the army or the people in Afghanistan who he liked helping. He just decided to work hard and get walking again on new robot legs and learn to use his new robot arm. And that way he could show other people that by working hard and staying positive, you can achieve anything.